CW00971203

A DEBT AGAINST THE LIVING

Thomas Jefferson famously wrote that the earth belongs to the living. His letter to James Madison is often quoted for the proposition that we should not be bound to the "dead hand of the past," suggesting that the Constitution should instead be interpreted as a living, breathing document. Less well known is Madison's response, in which he said the improvements made by the dead – including the U.S. Constitution – form a debt against the living, who benefit from them. In this illuminating book, Ilan Wurman introduces Madison's concept of originalism to a new generation and shows how it has shaped the U.S. Supreme Court in ways that are expected to continue following the death of Justice Antonin Scalia, one of the theory's leading proponents. It should be read by anyone seeking a better understanding of originalism and its ongoing influence on the constitutional jurisprudence of the Supreme Court.

Ilan Wurman is an attorney in Washington, DC, and a nonresident fellow at the Stanford Constitutional Law Center. He was formerly deputy general counsel on Senator Rand Paul's U.S. presidential campaign, associate counsel on Senator Tom Cotton's campaign for U.S. Senate, and a law clerk to the Honorable Jerry E. Smith of the U.S. Court of Appeals for the Fifth Circuit. His writing has appeared or is forthcoming in numerous law reviews, including the *Stanford Law Review* and the *Texas Law Review*, as well as in national journals, including *National Affairs*, *The Weekly Standard*, and *City Journal*. He graduated from Stanford Law School, and from Claremont McKenna College with degrees in government and physics.

A Debt Against the Living

AN INTRODUCTION TO ORIGINALISM

Ilan Wurman

CAMBRIDGE
UNIVERSITY PRESS

University Printing House, Cambridge CB2 8BS, United Kingdom

One Liberty Plaza, 20th Floor, New York, NY 10006, USA

477 Williamstown Road, Port Melbourne, VIC 3207, Australia

314-321, 3rd Floor, Plot 3, Splendor Forum, Jasola District Centre, New Delhi-110025, India

79 Anson Road, #06-04/06, Singapore 079906

Cambridge University Press is part of the University of Cambridge.

It furthers the University's mission by disseminating knowledge in the pursuit of education, learning and research at the highest international levels of excellence.

www.cambridge.org
Information on this title: www.cambridge.org/9781108419802
DOI: 10.1017/9781108304221

© Ilan Wurman 2017

First published 2017

A catalogue record for this publication is available from the British Library

Library of Congress Cataloging in Publication data
Names: Wurman, Ilan, 1987– author.
Title: A debt against the living : an introduction to originalism / Ilan Wurman,
Winston & Strawn LLP (Washington, DC).
Description: New York : Cambridge University Press, 2017. | Includes bibliographical
references and index.
Identifiers: LCCN 2017019181 | ISBN 9781108419802 (Hardback) |
ISBN 9781108412162 (Paperback)
Subjects: LCSH: Constitutional law–United States. | BISAC: LAW / General.
Classification: LCC KF4552 .W87 2017 | DDC 342.73001–dc23
LC record available at https://lccn.loc.gov/2017019181

ISBN 978-1-108-41980-2 Hardback
ISBN 978-1-108-41216-2 Paperback

To the memory of Justice Antonin Scalia.
And to his successor.

CONTENTS

FOREWORD

The presidency changes hands and the forces of political Washington (including much of the press and academia) shift positions on practically every question of structural constitutional law. Clinton to Bush, Bush to Obama, Obama to Trump. Opinions about executive power, checks and balances, the legitimacy of state obstruction of federal policy; opinions about undeclared wars, executive orders, signing statements, and presidential power over executive agencies; and opinions about filibusters, congressional oversight, the need to exhibit respect for the president or deference to his cabinet choices, who can sue to challenge executive action, and whether the president can independently interpret the Constitution: on all these issues, and more, political Washington has done U-turns with the caution of a teenage driver texting on his cell phone.

But the Constitution does not change. At least its words do not change: The Constitution means the same now, under President Trump, that it did under President Obama and President Bush – indeed that it has meant since the Founding. Can we agree on that?

Apparently not. Theorists on law school faculties have served as enablers to politicians on the courts to persuade us that the Constitution changes. It is a "Living Constitution," which unelected judges can infuse with meanings that no one ever saw in it before and no Constitutional Convention or ratifier ever thought they were enacting.

There is no more central question to our constitutional order: Does the Constitution have a fixed, objective, ascertainable meaning, applicable to the changing economic and social realities of succeeding generations? Or does a five-Justice majority of the Supreme Court have a legitimate right to read into the law its own notions of justice, equality, and social change?

This is the first book to explain to the ordinary citizen – free from what the late Justice Antonin Scalia called "jiggery pokery" – what it means to understand the Constitution as enduring law rather than politics by a different name. The author is a young gay conservative with an antipathy for party lines and a deep understanding of the need for a stable system of rights. He writes for his generation, but in a sense for all of us: all of us who distrust unbridled power, worry about the future, but trust in the capacity of the American republic to get through even the present times. The interpretive approach defended in this book is nuanced and modest. Many liberals and living constitutionalists will find its arguments compelling, and many self-styled "originalists" will find new and improved arguments for their own positions. This is a must-read book for any and all interested in the direction of law and the courts in the coming decades.

Yet the book is not just an abstract essay in how to interpret the Constitution. It is also an introduction to the Founding. As the book's introduction wonderfully illustrates, the Founders debated the nature of the Constitution and whether it would bind future generations. Thomas Jefferson famously wrote to his friend and political ally James Madison that the nation should have a constitutional revolution, or at a minimum constitutional revision and reform, every nineteen years. Madison broke with Jefferson on this point. Madison said instead that the constitutional order must be stable and long-lasting, giving rise to a kind of "debt" that the living have to the dead.

What is that debt against the living? Few modern Americans have more than the slightest acquaintance with the thought of the Founders. Who cares about a bunch of white guys (some of them slaveholders) who lived more than 200 years ago, in a world vastly different from our own? How can this very old Constitution possibly resolve any of the questions we have about government today? The answer is to recognize that the Constitution contains enduring principles of free government, and not a list of specific applications. When we face constitutional issues today, we do not ask what the Framers would have done. We ask what principles they enacted, and how those principles apply to the often very different circumstances now.

The Framers created a powerful new federal government – far more powerful than the Articles of Confederation that preceded it, and more powerful than some critics of government today wish to acknowledge. But the Framers did not make the central government all-powerful. Its powers are listed, defined, and limited; for the most part, noneconomic issues, often cultural in nature, are left to the various states. This division of authority enables different parts of the nation to preserve diverse ways of life. Utah does not have to be like California, or vice versa; efforts to nationalize decisions over educational content, marriage law, morals legislation, and the trade-off between state taxes and services threaten this diversity. Other issues – speech, religion, property, fair criminal procedure – are protected as a matter of individual right.

The most important matters are left to the democratic process: war, peace, taxes, spending, debt, and regulation are all left for the people themselves and their representatives to decide. Unlike some recently enacted constitutions around the world, which purport to compel action on such matters as health, education, environment, and poverty, our Constitution entrusts these questions to democratic deliberation and vote. If our elected leaders mess up the economy, it is their fault and ours – not the Constitution's. As Madison wrote (see Chapter 4), our Constitution – our "political experiment" – rests "on the capacity of mankind for self-government."

Even within the federal government, authority is carefully dispersed among competing institutions: the House of Representatives, the Senate, the president, and the judiciary. The Framers thus embedded within the powerful new federal government some internal checks against overreach. These checks and balances sometimes frustrate the quick fulfillment of political agendas (good and bad). This is often derided as "gridlock." The Framers, however, considered gridlock a feature, not a bug; they feared hasty and oppressive government action more than they feared the opposite.

Under this system, the President of the United States occupies a commanding position, to be sure. But he is subordinate to the law and often forced to compromise to accomplish his objectives. In particular, he cannot enact laws; only Congress can do that, subject to his veto. He cannot spend tax dollars on his own initiative, or borrow money on the credit of the United States without congressional approval, appoint officers to run the agencies of the federal government without Senatorial advice and consent (with a narrow exception for appointments during a recess), and he cannot start a war.

Yet during the last few decades, both Republican and Democratic presidents have stretched and maybe even breached these limits. President George W. Bush made sweeping claims of unilateral executive authority in the national security arena and asserted the power to override congressional statutes as Commander in Chief. President Obama launched an air war on Libya without congressional authorization, and attempted to rewrite the immigration laws by executive fiat when Congress refused to go along with his ideas. President Trump will likely be no more shy about flexing presidential muscles.

Judges in our system have two grave responsibilities. One is to uphold and enforce constitutional limits when they apply, even in the face of government power and popular opinion. The second is to stand back and allow democratic politics to govern when the Constitution is silent, even when the judge's own political preferences go the other way. The second is no less important than the first, and is often more difficult. This book lays out a way for judges to achieve both.

It is in times like these, where often our system of separation of powers seems to fall apart, where liberty seems to be threatened by a government that acts "outside the bounds of the Constitution," that we ought to reflect on the bedrock of our republican system of government. Against Jefferson's adolescent dream of creating government anew every generation, Madison argued the advantages of an enduring constitutional order. Ilan Wurman has rediscovered that argument, and presented it in a compelling form that speaks to us today.

Michael W. McConnell
Richard and Frances Mallery
Professor of Law,
Stanford Law School
May 1, 2017

ACKNOWLEDGMENTS

Whom does one acknowledge after writing a book like this? There are too many people – too many whose great wisdom and insight have shaped my thinking over the last decade as I studied the Founders, their bequest to us in the Constitution, and their significance to modern legal thought. There are too many people who should have written this book instead, and who would have written it far better. Much of what I say here is due to the influence of these scholars, teachers, mentors, and friends.

Although many contributed to my thinking over the years, and many others contributed specifically to this book by reviewing parts of the manuscript, I owe a special thanks Michael McConnell and William Baude, under whom I studied for three years as a law student. They encouraged this project, shaped my thinking, and even read and reread parts or all of this book. I know they disagree with some of what I say here. Much insight I owe to them, and where I am wrong is surely where I have failed to heed their advice. Any such errors are truly my own.

Parts of this book have also appeared in varied forms over the last few years, whether in law reviews or more popular journals. I have noted these in the relevant parts, and I thank these journals for letting me reuse my prior work where appropriate. I also wish to thank George Thomas, who commented on an earlier draft and encouraged me to seek out academic publishers, and Camille Peeples for her helpful research assistance.

Finally I must acknowledge my parents, Hadassah and Ze'ev, whose love and support make everything possible. And especially my father, who, although his training and career is in electrical engineering, somehow always manages to read everything I write and provide insightful comments.

INTRODUCTION

"[T]he earth belongs to the living, and not to the dead ..."
Thomas Jefferson, Letter to James Madison (1789)

"The *improvements* made by the dead form a debt against
the living ..."
James Madison, Letter to Thomas Jefferson (1790)

Why does one generation, long dead and gone, have a right to bind another? Thomas Jefferson famously made this argument in a 1789 letter to James Madison: "I set out on this ground which I suppose to be self evident," Jefferson wrote from revolutionary Paris, "'*that the earth belongs in usufruct to the living*;' that the dead have neither powers nor rights over it. . . . [B]y the law of nature, one generation is to another as one independent nation to another."[1] This letter from Jefferson is well known: it is often quoted for the proposition that we should not be bound by the "dead hand of the past," that a constitution that is not a "living, breathing document" is not a legitimate constitution worthy of our obedience today.

Eminent law professors in illustrious law journals have repeated this argument for decades. David Strauss of the University of Chicago has paraphrased the Jeffersonian problem as follows:

> Why do we care about the Framers of the Constitution? After all, they lived long ago, in a world that was different in countless ways from ours. Why does it matter what their views were, for any reasons other than purely historical ones? And if we don't care about the Framers, why do we care about their handiwork, the Constitution itself? It was the product of the Framers' times and the Framers' sensibilities. What possible reason can we have for allowing its provisions to rule us today?[2]

1

"Originalists," Strauss writes elsewhere, "do not have an answer to
Jefferson's question: why should we allow people who lived long ago, in
a different world, to decide fundamental questions about our government and society today?"[3] Strauss comes up with an answer, but one
that altogether avoids the question. We don't really follow what the
Framers thought anyway, so it's no big deal; and those parts we do
follow, we do so because it's important to "settle" questions even if
they aren't settled right. But according to Strauss, there is no better
reason compelling us to obey the Constitution, and if we didn't already
ignore much of what the Founders thought or expected, there'd be
even less reason to obey it.

Paul Brest, a former dean of Stanford Law School, wrote in a
famous article that "[e]ven if the adopters freely consented to the
Constitution," that "is not an adequate basis for continuing fidelity to
the founding document, for their consent cannot bind succeeding
generations." He declared: "We did not adopt the Constitution, and
those who did are dead and gone."[4] Many libertarians also agree with
Jefferson's principle that we cannot be bound by the dead hand of the
past because *we* – the current, living generation – never consented to be
governed by the Constitution.[5]

Some authors have written particularly incendiary articles impugning
our Constitution. In one entitled "Burn the Constitution," a left-wing
author wrote in *Jacobin*, "It is a measure of our current ideological
morass that liberals, in their own enlightened and open-minded way,
still masochistically embrace a throne-and-altar orthodoxy that subor-
dinates the people's will to a virtually unalterable diktat handed down by
an ancient council of aristocratic, semi-deified lawgivers."[6] Georgetown
law professor Louis Seidman wrote in the *New York Times* only a few
years ago that we should "give up on the Constitution."[7] University of
Texas law professor Sandy Levinson wrote in his book *Our Undemocratic
Constitution* that the Constitution is deeply flawed and should be abandoned. It is "insufficiently democratic" and "dysfunctional," we should
"no longer express our blind devotion to it," and we should reject it in
favor of a new constitutional convention.[8] In his one-page prelude, he
quotes at length Jefferson's "dead-hand" letter.

Many, in other words, have heard of Jefferson's letter, and it has
come to symbolize a potent criticism of interpreting the Constitution as

it was originally understood and of the Constitution itself. It has come to represent the notion that the Constitution is woefully outdated and should not be binding upon us today. Fewer have heard James Madison's response to Jefferson. But his response makes a powerful case for constitutional obedience. Every generation is necessarily dependent on the previous generations that have cultivated its inheritance, he wrote:

> If the earth be the gift of *nature* to the living, their title can extend to the earth in its *natural* state only. The *improvements* made by the dead form a debt against the living, who take the benefit of them. This debt cannot be otherwise discharged than by a proportionate obedience to the will of the Authors of the improvements.[9]

That statement seems remarkable: Does the Constitution truly create a debt against those who live today so that we must – or we ought to – follow the will of its authors? Is the Constitution an "improvement" of the kind justifying our continuing obedience?

Who is right: Thomas Jefferson or James Madison? This book answers in favor of Madison. It aims to arm the reader with basic arguments about the legitimacy of our Constitution and our Founding, and to explain the relevance of these arguments to modern debates over constitutional interpretation. It argues that the Constitution does form a debt against us – against the living generation – that compels us to continue to obey and abide by it today. It then argues that originalism, the idea that the Constitution should be interpreted as it was originally understood by the Framers who wrote it and the public that ratified it, is the only method of constitutional interpretation that faithfully discharges this debt. This book is a short introduction to, and defense of, originalism and the Founding.

The stakes could not be greater. How we interpret the Constitution and whether or not our government takes seriously its boundaries have extraordinary implications for human liberty and flourishing. We live under an enormous and ever-growing administrative state that, many argue, governs outside the bounds of the Constitution. Government agencies often centralize legislative, executive, and judicial power within their hands. States and localities have become submerged under an ever-growing federal government that appears to transgress the original limits of the Constitution.

This shift in the way we govern ourselves has been justified for several decades on the ground that the Constitution is a "living, breathing" document that allows for such updating in the modern age. And indeed, constitutional law legitimizes such government actions that originally would have been understood to be unconstitutional by developing modern doctrines and interpretations through which the Supreme Court declares them constitutional. In the coming years, the President of the United States will quite likely have the opportunity to appoint a handful of Supreme Court justices who may determine the path of constitutional law for decades to come. All Americans must therefore understand the case for why our Constitution, as it was originally understood, is a legitimate document worthy of our obedience today. And all should strive to understand how we ought to interpret the Constitution to be consistent with its original principles.

The argument and organization of the book are as follows. The first chapter briefly explores the origins of originalism and why it matters today. It explains some terms and other background. It shows how originalism, if we fully commit to it, could lead to a dramatically different constitutional order than the one currently existing. But we won't have established why originalism is correct, or why we should even care about what the Constitution says – that is, why we should obey it in the first place.

The next few chapters establish the case for originalism and the Constitution. Madison's answer to Jefferson suggests there are two inquiries: Does the Constitution create a debt against the living? That is, is it binding on us? And if so, how do we faithfully discharge that debt – by Madison's originalism, or something else? I will suggest that to answer these questions it makes more sense to take them in reverse order. After all, to know whether the Constitution is binding on us today, we first have to know what it actually says or does. And to know that, I will argue, we have to be originalists. Only after we know what the Constitution says or does can we investigate whether what it says is *good* – that is, whether it continues to form a debt against the living.

Chapter 2 addresses the first inquiry. What does the Constitution *say*, or more accurately, how do we figure out what it says? This chapter draws on current legal scholarship to introduce what we might call the linguistic theory of originalism. How do we interpret *any* text intended for a public audience? How do we interpret a fried chicken recipe from the eighteenth century, or a law enacted in the 1800s? We don't use hidden meanings, nor do we change meaning over time to suit different purposes; we interpret any such written (or oral) text by the public meaning it originally had when it was written (or spoken). We have to be originalists because all such texts *must* be interpreted that way. That's just how our system of language works.

Now, that's not to say that all legal systems have to give *legal effect* to this original public meaning. We could have a legal system in which the meaning of the words isn't binding or in which the legal effect of the words departs significantly from original meaning. For example, we could have a system in which all statutes merely "guide" the discretion of judges, who are required to do "justice" as they understand it in any case that comes before them. But this isn't how we do things, and there are entirely good reasons why: over the thousand or so years in which English and American law has developed, our system has concluded that "rule of law" values such as stability, predictability, consistency, and fairness are served by treating the meaning of the words as authoritative – or at least paramount.

This theory of originalism thus answers one of two questions: How should we *interpret* the Constitution? It does not, however, answer our second, equally important question: *Why* should we obey the Constitution at all? We may all agree that we have to be originalists because the theory of language – and the role of text in our legal system – demands it. But then we might decide that the Constitution as originally understood is a bad Constitution; perhaps we don't like what it says. This approach to originalism tells us nothing about constitutional legitimacy.

Chapters 3 and 4 seek an answer to this second question: Is the Constitution a *good* constitution worthy of our continued obedience today? Chapter 3 begins by surveying three popular theories of constitutional legitimacy that have influenced the public debate. We might label these theories as "libertarian," "progressive," and "conservative." The libertarian theory argues that the Constitution is legitimate and binding because it protects our natural rights. The progressive theory argues that it is legitimate because it allows for contemporary updating and responsiveness to modern social movements. The conservative theory argues that the Constitution is legitimate because it was rooted in an act of popular sovereignty – because "we the people" voted to ratify the Constitution in 1789, and therefore it remains good law to this day.

Which of these theories is persuasive? By examining them we might find the elements of truth in each one. We might tease out the right and wrong. We then compare these theories, in Chapter 4, to what our Founders thought. Why did *they* think the Constitution was worthy of our obedience? Why did James Madison believe that it could form a debt against the living generation?

As we shall see, the Founders thought our Constitution was worthy of our reverence and obedience because it was legitimate in much broader ways than many of the modern originalist theories suppose. Our Constitution is not legitimate only because it protects natural rights, only because it creates a republican form of government, or only because it was ratified by an act of popular sovereignty; the Constitution has to be legitimate in *all* three ways for it to bind us.

But each of these grounds for constitutional obedience might be fatally flawed. The Constitution does not perfectly protect natural rights, does not create a perfect republican form of government, and was not enacted in a perfect act of popular sovereignty. Yet James Madison and others argued that the Constitution is still worthy of our obedience because, even if it is imperfectly legitimate in these three important ways, it is *sufficiently* legitimate in each way that prudence demands our continuing adherence to the whole. We will explore what the Founders had in mind when they discussed prudence as a political principle. It is here that we will study Madison's response to Jefferson.

We will thus have answered both questions in our inquiry. We can conclude that we must be originalists because the nature of language and our legal system require it, and that the original Constitution is legitimate and worthy of our obedience because we like what it says. The remainder of the book confronts more particular, and quite interesting, problems in originalism. Chapter 5 addresses how originalism actually works in practice. What happens when originalism supplies more than one plausible answer? It is at this point that many originalists concede that interpretation "runs out." Originalism only gets us so far. After interpretation runs out, they argue, we enter the realm of *construction* – what do we do then? Perhaps unsurprisingly, there's some disagreement.

Libertarians tend to favor a "presumption of liberty" construction, whereby each government action must be justified as necessary and proper and is presumed to be unconstitutional if it infringes on liberty. The more conservative originalist theories maintain that the Constitution should be construed with a "presumption of constitutionality": government acts should be presumed constitutional unless they clearly infringe on protected rights. Others claim there is no difference between interpretation and construction at all. Which of these understandings is correct? Which of these does the Constitution enshrine in its broad strokes?

Chapter 6 addresses the prevalent criticism that originalism's reliance on history is fatal to it. It first addresses whether history is too indeterminate to provide us with satisfactory answers. It then confronts one of the greatest criticisms of originalism – that lawyers just aren't good at doing history – and makes the case for why lawyers *can* and *should* do history. We shall see how history provides us with useful knowledge and how that knowledge can be deployed in constitutional cases.

Chapter 7 then confronts head-on whether originalism can justify *Brown v. Board of Education*. Many nonoriginalists argue that if originalism can't justify *Brown*, then originalism has an uphill battle to fight. I think they are right. Originalism must result in mostly the right answers, which is merely another way of saying the original Constitution must be on the whole just. But I think it does get at the right answers. Originalism can – and does – justify *Brown*. We will use *Brown* as a case study in originalism and observe how different theories of originalism approach and answer the question. Our original Constitution – the Constitution with all subsequent Amendments as they were originally understood – continues to be just and worthy of our obedience today.

The book ends with a brief coda on nonoriginalist theories, the most common of which is often referred to as "living constitutionalism." Justice Scalia famously quipped that originalism doesn't have to be perfect: It doesn't have to outrun the bear; it just has to run faster than any other available theory. And, he claimed, it outruns nonoriginalists who don't have a theory at all. But I would say that that is not quite right. Nonoriginalists do have a variety of theories, some of which are quite interesting. Understanding these theories will help strengthen our case for originalism itself, which does have some real running to do.

Examining nonoriginalism might also lead us to a perhaps startling conclusion: much less separates the best originalists from the best living constitutionalists than is often imagined. So to my liberal readers, take heart! You might find that originalism as it is now understood is quite an attractive theory. One of this book's objectives is to reveal just how capacious a proper understanding of originalism is. Originalists recognize that original meaning often *requires* that the application of the text evolve as modern circumstances evolve; more still, they often recognize that originalism doesn't always lead to specific answers, but rather to a range of plausible answers. Conversely, living constitutionalists almost universally agree that the text and its original meaning matter in constitutional interpretation – even though they think original meaning is less determinate than originalists tend to think and that it should be less dispositive.

Originalism is, to be sure, a complex theory. Its proponents disagree over dozens of issues and nuances. It is often said that originalism, like the common law, is still "working itself pure." There remains disagreement, for example, over what originalism *is*, with some originalists looking to the original public meaning of the Constitution and others to the meaning it would have to a hypothetical reasonable observer. The justifications for originalism, and the implications its advocates draw from it, are even more numerous and sometimes conflicting. That there are many nuances over which originalists disagree, however, does not mean originalism cannot be distilled into a few key findings or conclusions. It is those findings, and those conclusions, that this book seeks to uncover.

PART I

Preliminaries and Language

1 THE ORIGINS OF ORIGINALISM

"Those who framed the Constitution chose their words carefully; they debated at great length the minutest points. The language they chose meant something."[1]

Attorney General Edwin Meese (1985)

IN THE BEGINNING

Some of you might already be thinking: When was originalism ever not a thing? Originalism is quite a commonsensical idea, after all. It has many flavors, but we can define it broadly as the idea that the Constitution should be interpreted as its words were originally understood by the Framers who wrote the Constitution in 1787 and by the public that ratified it between 1787 and 1789. More broadly still, it is the idea that words have an original public meaning at the time they were spoken or written and presented to the world.

Don't we interpret all human communication like that? Doesn't that just, well, make sense? If we change the meaning of the words over time, aren't we just making things up as we go along? The short answer is yes. But not everyone always saw things this way.

Starting in the 1950s, America witnessed a revolution in its constitutional jurisprudence. The Supreme Court, ushered by Chief Justice Earl Warren, began discovering in the Constitution rights and powers no one had ever thought were there. The Court created whole new sets of rights for criminal defendants, including the *Miranda* rights popularized by television.[2] It required states to suppress evidence

11

as a remedy for unlawful police conduct.[3] Conservatives feared that criminal defendants for whom there was plenty of evidence to convict were let free based on judicially created rights nowhere found in the text of the Constitution. In 1971, they were given a powerful voice by San Francisco's renegade police officer, Harry ("Dirty Harry") Callahan, memorably played by Clint Eastwood. The district attorney refused to prosecute a serial killer because the evidence against him was obtained through a warrantless search and, shall we say, Dirty Harry's less than kosher interrogation tactics (outside the presence of a lawyer, no less!). The evidence was thus inadmissible, and the killer would walk. "I'm all broken up about that man's rights," Dirty Harry declares sarcastically. "It's the law," says the DA, defending the suppression of the gun and the confession. Dirty Harry retorts, "Well then the law is crazy!"

And then just two years after Dirty Harry enthralled his audiences, the Court in *Roe v. Wade* constitutionalized the right to an abortion in accordance with what the Justices labeled the "penumbras" of other constitutional rights. This revolution crystallized the opposition to what has become known in some quarters as judicial activism. The term "activism" suggests that the Supreme Court had been doing something wrong. Wasn't the Court simply making things up as it went along? Where in the text were all of these rights? That the Court had to invent "penumbras" in which to find them seemed to give away the whole game.

But what was the alternative? By what principles could those who opposed the Court's decisions claim that the Court was wrong? One answer is intuitive, almost obvious: What about just following what the text *says*? Surely the text doesn't answer *every* question, and perhaps the text can be ambiguous, but can't we all agree that at least nothing in the Constitution says anything about abortion? That nothing in the Constitution requires the suppression of evidence when officers commit constitutional violations? That nothing in the Constitution says a police officer can't ask a criminal suspect questions? (The Fifth Amendment protects a witness from being compelled to *testify* against himself in court, not necessarily from having to answer to police questioning.[4])

There is another possible answer. Can't we agree that the Constitution was never *intended* – by those who wrote it, or perhaps by those who ratified it in the state conventions – to have the effect given it by the Warren Court? Did the Founders ever *intend* that the federal government grow as big as it has? That the Congress would delegate its legislative powers to unelected federal officials in a giant administrative bureaucracy?

Reagan's attorney general, Edwin Meese, suggested this answer in a renowned speech to the American Bar Association in 1985.[5] Reflecting on the end of the Supreme Court's latest term, he wrote, "The voting blocs, the arguments, all reveal a greater allegiance to what the Court thinks constitutes sound public policy than a deference to what the Constitution – its text and intention – may demand." What should replace this ad hoc, protean approach to constitutional law? "What, then, should a constitutional jurisprudence actually be?" Meese asked.

> It should be a jurisprudence of original intention. By seeking to judge policies in light of principles, rather than remold principles in light of policies, the Court could avoid both the charge of incoherence *and* the charge of being either too conservative or too liberal.
>
> A jurisprudence seriously aimed at the explication of original intention would produce defensible principles of government that would not be tainted by ideological predilection. This belief in a jurisprudence of original intention also reflects a deeply rooted commitment to the idea of democracy. The Constitution represents the consent of the governed to the structures and powers of the government. The Constitution is the fundamental will of the people; that is why it is the fundamental law. To allow the courts to govern simply by what it views at the time as fair and decent is a scheme of government no longer popular; the idea of democracy has suffered. The permanence of the Constitution has been weakened. A constitution that is viewed as only what the judges say it is no longer is a constitution in the true sense.
>
> Those who framed the Constitution chose their words carefully; they debated at great length the minutest points. The language they chose meant something. It is incumbent upon the Court to determine what that meaning was. This is not a shockingly new theory; nor is it arcane or archaic.

Originalism did not originate with Attorney General Ed Meese. Robert Bork – whose Supreme Court nomination was infamously derailed – is credited with having first advanced the theory in the modern age in a 1971 law review article in which he similarly remarked that "[a] persistently disturbing aspect of constitutional law is its lack of theory." The courts, he wrote, "are without effective criteria and, therefore we have come to expect that the nature of the Constitution will change, often quite dramatically, as the personnel of the Supreme Court changes."[6]

New Justices pour their own particular values into the Constitution, Bork wrote. But if the constitutional text itself does not specify which value is to be preferred, how can the Justices decide that their particular values are what should govern? One principled way to decide is to "take from the document rather specific values that text or history show the framers actually to have intended and which are capable of being translated into principled rules."[7]

It is somewhat odd to have to credit Bork with originating originalism. We've already hinted at why: Isn't originalism just obvious? Perhaps we shouldn't go that far, but originalism is certainly intuitive. And, indeed, most lawyers and judges until the early twentieth century interpreted all legal texts, including the Constitution, in much this same way: by looking at the intention of a law's authors. Or more specifically, by looking at their intentions as evidenced by the words they used and normal conventions of usage, grammar, syntax, and other conventional legal tools of interpretation.

But we had mostly forgotten about this way of doing things in the era of progressivism and legal "realism." Law professors began teaching in the early 1900s that judges by necessity *make* law, rather than discern or interpret law, based on their own, unconscious sociological predispositions. Judges, the realist will say, cannot divorce their own values from the law, and so they have no choice but to pour those values into the law. So the judges *have* to make things up as they go along – or at least, judges have always done so, and they always will.

Robert Bork was the first to intuit that we had strayed from a rather obvious path of believing that words have meaning and judges can discern those meanings. Judges will always have predispositions and background assumptions, of course, but surely that can't mean that *anything* goes. Attorney General Meese made it the purpose of Reagan's Justice Department to return to this rather commonsense path of legal interpretation.

THE PROGRESSIVE COUNTERATTACK

Then came the progressive counterattack. Supreme Court Justice William Brennan responded a few months after Meese's speech with one of his own at Georgetown University.[8] He ascribed arrogance to a judicial philosophy of original intention. How can we possibly discern what the Founders thought about the particular cases that come before the Court today? "We current Justices read the Constitution in the only way that we can: as twentieth century Americans," Brennan claimed. Yes, we often look to the history of the framing, he continued,

> [b]ut the ultimate question must be: What do the words of the text mean in our time? For the genius of the Constitution rests not in any static meaning it might have had in a world that is dead and gone, but in the adaptability of its great principles to cope with current problems and current needs.

That's fair enough. There's no doubt that there is much compelling about Justice Brennan's account. How could the Founders have known about peculiarly modern-day problems? Shouldn't we adapt their principles to cope with current conditions? But as we shall see through-out this book, Brennan's response assumes many untrue things about originalism. Surely the great principles have to be adapted to current needs – but doesn't the text of the Constitution already permit such adapting? And doesn't it do so in a way that also maintains certain limits? The First Amendment applies to the Internet, no one can seriously disagree with that; but does that mean that Supreme Court Justices get to decide that capital punishment is cruel and unusual in violation of the Eighth Amendment – or perhaps more accurately in violation of the "evolving standards of decency that mark the progress of a maturing society" – even though capital crimes are explicitly contemplated in other parts of the Constitution?[9]

We must be fair to Justice Brennan, of course. The originalism to which he was responding was in an incipient stage. Its advocates had not yet perfected the theory (and they still haven't today, I might add, as we shall see throughout this book). But Brennan nicely sets up the impetus, the motivation behind the competition to originalism that we shall take up in the final chapter: Isn't originalism too rigid?

Why do we care about what the Founders really thought since their world is "dead and gone"?

Paul Brest, who would later become the dean of Stanford Law School, wrote a few years earlier what has come to be considered a fatal attack on originalism at least in its early form. In his famous article, "The Misconceived Quest for the Original Understanding,"[10] Brest sought to undermine the notion that there is such a thing as the Founders' collective "intent" vis-à-vis any particular constitutional provision. How do you determine a collective intent for a body like the Constitutional Convention? What if various Framers thought different things about the same provision? What if they did not even think about how the text they were writing would be applied to particular problems? Whose intent counts?

Adding to this attack was H. Jefferson Powell's famous article in 1985, "The Original Understanding of Original Intent,"[11] which argued that the Founders themselves did not intend for their intentions to govern the future. How then can a jurisprudence of original intentions be internally consistent? If you want to abide by the Founders' intent but they intended that you *not* do just that, one can't really be an original-intent originalist.

There is much wisdom in what Brest and Powell said, and so originalism adapted to accommodate their arguments. Although both Powell and Brest described more plausible versions of originalism – those that looked to high-level purposes rather than to the specific intent of any particular Framer and that sought original meaning through words, grammar, context, and legal interpretive conventions – most originalists up to that time had focused on the original "intent" of the Framers. After the Brest-Powell onslaught, they quickly adopted a new version of originalism: the original public understanding.

The original public understanding version maintains that the meaning of a constitutional provision is the meaning the public that ratified the Constitution would have understood it to have. It does not depend on the secret intentions of the Founding Fathers. It does not even depend on the collective intentions of the various ratifying conventions. It asks, how would the people have understood the written words of the Constitution they were adopting? What would they have understood it to be accomplishing? That means we have to understand not only the way words were used but also the purpose for which the words were deployed, the social context, and so on.

Many problems were thus solved, but the debate over originalism has continued. Originalism, I mentioned earlier, is often described as a theory that is still "working itself pure" – an expression Lord Mansfield used to describe the common law and its piecemeal, precedential, evolutionary progression.[12] Some would say that the theory of originalism evolved from an "original public understanding" version to an "original public meaning" version. I'm not sure I see a difference. Surely the ratifying public (or at least its informed readers) would have "understood" the Constitution by the "meaning" of its words. Either label clarifies what is going on: the meaning of the Constitution is best discerned by its words in the linguistic, historical, and social context, and those words and that context are public and not secret.

Original public understanding or meaning might still have some problems. What if different segments of the public did or would have understood the text differently? What if most people were politically ignorant and really didn't know much about the constitutional text at all? Leading originalists today have thus suggested that the original public understanding should aim at what a *hypothetical reasonable observer*, someone fully informed about the history and context of various constitutional provisions and skilled in linguistic conventions, would have understood.[13] Even this method might still reveal disagreements over meaning, of course, but that merely suggests we need ways to resolve indeterminacies, which we shall discuss a bit later in this book. It hardly suggests that no meaning exists at all, or that there aren't tools for deciding which meaning we go with when there are plausible alternative understandings.

We need not get more bogged down than this. We see clearly enough that, although originalism is not a settled theory, it has been and continues to be refined by legal thinkers. When someone says – as even some law professors still do – that "originalism refutes originalism"[14] because the Founders themselves weren't originalist (citing H. Jefferson Powell's article), you can respond that original *intentions* originalism has been severely challenged but that original public understanding originalism has survived the unrelenting counteroffensive.

NO MORE INTENT?

The history just described raises some interesting questions. Although we will touch on some of them elsewhere in the book, we may benefit from introducing them now. First, what is the role of intent, now that "original intentions" or "original intent" are some kind of dirty words? With few exceptions, almost no one today defends original intent originalism.[15] Many originalists even suggest we should not look at James Madison's convention notes because they only tell us the specific intent of a few Framers.[16]

Is it really true that intent does not matter at all? Surely it matters somewhat. Now, we have to be clear about just what we mean by intent. Do we have to count up the "intention votes" of all the delegates to the Constitutional Convention and ask whether more thought X about a particular part of the text than thought Y about that text? No. But surely we can look at the overarching *purposes* of the Constitution to get at some kind of collective intent. Surely it helps us to know that the purpose of the Constitution was both to enable democracy as well as to serve as a check on the excesses of democracy. Surely it helps us to know that the Framers were overwhelmingly concerned with giving energy to the executive, but only as far as republican principles would admit. It helps us to know the *general* intent of the Founding Fathers.

Historians seek this kind of "intent" all the time. What were Caesar's motives when he crossed the Rubicon? What was the Roman Senate thinking when it declared him perpetual dictator? What was Lincoln hoping to accomplish by fighting the civil war – saving the Union, abolishing slavery, abetting northern industrial interests? What was the Athenian assembly hoping to accomplish by initially sentencing the citizens of Mytilene to death? We ask questions about historical and collective intent all the time.

Consider also a classic case of statutory interpretation. The great William Blackstone described a Bolognian law declaring "that whoever drew blood in the streets should be punished with the utmost severity."[17] A surgeon comes to the aid of a man who has fallen in a fit, and cuts open his veins. (Let us assume that this was the standard of care in medieval Bologna.) Has the surgeon violated the prohibition? Well, it would *seem* that he has: he has quite literally "drawn blood in the streets." But don't we know what the lawgivers really intended here? Don't we know that they meant to prevent fighting on the street, not to prevent doctors from saving lives? The jurists concluded that the surgeon had not violated the prohibition.

So intent at a high level of generality, perhaps better described as purpose, tells us a lot. Purpose or intent helps us choose between two possible interpretations of a statute: we should quite obviously choose the interpretation consistent with the general purpose behind the law. But someone might object that in the above example there really weren't two plausible interpretations. The law was clear. The question rather was whether the statute, which literally applied to the situation, should be construed not to apply anyway because it is inconsistent with purpose. Put another way, can purpose sometimes override plain statutory text?

Many would say yes, but only where the application of the literal meaning would be "absurd." Usually the argument goes something like this: "The legislature couldn't possibly have intended that outcome, for it would be absurd, and so we shouldn't apply the rule." This is usually called the absurdity doctrine. But why have one at all? Precisely because words only have meaning in context, and the context includes the intent with which the words are communicated.

There is a neat schema in the academic literature, called the *funnel of abstraction*, that helps crystallize the point. Think of a reverse pyramid (i.e., a funnel), where at the point we have the text. That is the most concrete – the least abstract – datum to which we look to discern meaning. One rung higher on the funnel is the slightly more abstract notion of the specific intent of particular lawgivers, and even more abstract is the general intent or perhaps purpose for which the legislation was passed. If we go even higher, we might have some background principles of law that we look to. These constitute the most abstract rung on the funnel of abstraction.[18]

As one goes up and down the funnel of abstraction, the textual meaning becomes clearer. Suppose we can know the meaning of a word to within a five-degree angle of certainty. One might then look at linguistic conventions, or legislative intent, or statutory purpose, and so forth to see if there are any clues that sharpen our degree of certainty. An analysis of context or purpose might reduce our uncertainty to but a one-degree angle. We are pretty sure we know what "draw blood on the streets" means, but as we go up higher and higher and then back down along the funnel of abstraction, we better understand what the words mean.

INTERPRETATION AND CONSTRUCTION

To be sure, perhaps this approach makes "meaning" do too much work. After all, can we really say the no-blood-on-the-streets statute "means" there is an exception for doctors? Maybe not. Another way to look at this issue, which is probably a bit more precise, is to recognize that sometimes we can know everything about the "meaning" of a text and it *still doesn't answer our legal question.* For example, a statute might say, "killing another human being is a crime." Does that mean there is no exception for self-defense? That there is no insanity defense? Does it tell us anything about attempts or conspiracy to commit murder? Our statute "means" one thing, but its *legal effect* might go beyond that meaning because of other legal rules that already exist in the legal system – such as rules for self-defense, insanity, attempt, and conspiracy. It may be that there is a valid existing rule providing for exceptions to statutes in emergency situations – and hence our doctor can draw blood on the streets.[19] Thus, it can be consistent with originalism to override the clear meaning of any one legal text in light of other preexisting legal rules in the legal system, such as those providing for exceptions in emergency or absurd situations.

Now, what if we've looked at text, history, purpose, and so on, as well as the effect of the other legal rules in the system, and the answer still isn't clear? What if we have done all the *interpretation* we can do, and the answer is that this piece of legislation *might* be unconstitutional, but it is just as likely that it's constitutional? In the academic lingo, what happens when interpretation "runs out"?

Many originalists would say that we must then enter the realm of *construction.* Originalism may permit a range of plausible meanings. What we do within that range might have to be external to the text. Perhaps at this point we throw up our hands and say we presume the legislation to be constitutional. Or maybe we say if the government can't prove that it's constitutional, we should presume that liberty prevails. Maybe we say that in a contest between states' rights and the enumerated federal powers, all else being equal, the states win.

The different theories of originalism we will discuss in the coming chapters adopt different "constructions" along these lines. As we shall see, there are complications. Many advocates of these various "constructions" seem to claim that they are mandated by the Constitution's text. If that's true, then they aren't really constructions, but rather just part of interpretation. Indeed, some originalist theorists suggest that there is no real difference between interpretation and construction. We shall try to evaluate who is right as we go.

LEGITIMACY AND THE FIRST ORIGINALISTS

Attorney General Meese's remarks point to another issue that is a main thrust of this book: the question of constitutional legitimacy. Originalism was initially justified, including in Meese's view, on the ground that it is the only theory consistent with the legitimacy of a *democratic* Constitution. We live in a democracy, and so we the people get to decide important public policy questions through our elected representatives, except where we the people have already decided to keep such power from our legislators in the Constitution. And what we the people decided to withhold from our government is what we originally intended to withhold or understood to be withholding. Surely judges who pour their own values into the Constitution are not better spokesmen for we the people?

So at least the early originalists believed that we had to be originalist because that was the only way the Constitution would be legitimate. But most modern-day originalists don't think like that. Some claim that we have to be originalists because the "writtenness" of the Constitution requires it. Others say that there is simply no other way to interpret *any* communication, whether written or oral. We might refine this point by stating that our legal system by default gives legal effect to the original public meaning of a law's words. In which case, we aren't originalists because only originalism is consistent with a legitimate constitution; rather, we are originalists because that's how our system of language and law works.

The question of what makes the Constitution legitimate is then separate. Once we interpret the Constitution with its original public meaning, do we find that it is legitimate and worthy of our obedience? If so, is it because we decide that the Constitution protects natural rights? Is it because it creates a genuine democracy? We shall take up these questions shortly.

AN ORIGINALIST AMERICA

Those are the issues with which the history of originalism has had to contend. Before we contend with them ourselves, let us pause to consider why this debate is important from a practical perspective. It should be obvious by now that it is important from a theoretical perspective: If the Constitution isn't legitimate, why bother with what it says?

But the practical side of things is just as significant. How different would constitutional law look today if we were all hard-core, full-fledged originalists? There are at least three highly significant bodies of law that may have to change. To start, some of the New Deal State would have to be limited. The federal government today legislates in almost all areas of life on the grounds that it is regulating interstate commerce. Federal minimum wage laws, federal labor standards, and federal welfare programs are all justified under the commerce clause.

As originally understood by the founding generation, however, commerce meant something narrower: the exchange of goods.[20] It did not encompass, say, the manufacturing of goods within purely local dimensions. Because Congress only has power to regulate commerce and possibly to facilitate it,[21] minimum wage laws and other labor regulations might have to be left to the states. It means most welfare programs likely have to be left to the states. Much of what the federal government does today it would likely be unable to do under an originalist interpretation of the Constitution. I heard a story that once Judge Douglas Ginsburg of the U.S. Court of Appeals for the District of Columbia Circuit was told by a Justice Department attorney that, under the judge's interpretation of the Constitution, he would have to undo all of the New Deal State. Judge Ginsburg quipped: "So much to do, so little time."

Second, some administrative law would have to be revised. The original Constitution never contemplated that government agencies would wield legislative, executive, and judicial power. The Constitution creates a very specific government structure whereby only the Congress could exercise the legislative power, only the president and his officials could exercise the executive power, and only judges appointed by the president with tenure and salary protections could exercise the judicial power. Agencies never had the constitutional authority to exercise at least two of these powers, let alone *all three of them at once*. And yet constitutional law today allows bureaucrats to do just that.*

Third, as already suggested, much criminal defense law might have to be changed. *Miranda*, at a minimum, would have to be reversed. Police would not have to tell a suspect he has the right to remain silent. Violations of the Fourth Amendment's right to be free from unreasonable searches and seizures probably would not require the suppression of evidence. That's not to say all of these constitutional doctrines are bad from a policy perspective – only that at least some of them are hard to justify on originalist grounds. That's also not to say Congress could not mandate them if it chose to do so. (Indeed, I suspect that Congress *would* enact many of the criminal procedure protections of modern Supreme Court doctrine.)

Some originalists (especially the libertarian ones) also claim that, as originally understood, the Fourteenth Amendment's guarantee to each citizen the "privileges" and "immunities" of citizenship meant that the states could not infringe on economic liberties without compelling justifications.[22] And yet most states infringe frequently on economic freedom by, for example, requiring licenses to engage in normal occupations.

---

* The doctrine that allows them to do so is called the "nondelegation" doctrine. It holds that, so long as Congress gives the agencies an "intelligible principle," the agencies can make rules governing our everyday conduct. Congress has delegated responsibility to the agencies for the making of hundreds of thousands of rules, all of which have the force of law. Thus, the agencies exercise legislative power. These same agencies, as arms of the executive branch, often enforce their own rules in their own tribunals with their own administrative law judges. You see the problem. An unelected branch of government – not even the president himself – is wielding legislative, executive, and judicial power all at once. James Madison once defined tyranny as the combination of these powers in a single body.

To be sure, not all originalists want to go as far as what these points suggest. Originalists do have various theories of precedent.[23] They have theories as to why we ought to respect certain unoriginalist constitutional doctrines but not others. But the important point here is that originalism *matters*. It makes a difference. And taken all the way, it can work a radical transformation in the way we interpret the Constitution. So let us now turn to the case for originalism.

2 THE MEANING OF MEANING

"Interpreting the Constitution is no more difficult, and no
different in principle, than interpreting a late-eighteenth-century
recipe for fried chicken."[1]

Gary Lawson (1997)

Most originalists accept that the question of *how* we should interpret
the Constitution is separate from the question of *whether* the Constitution is legitimate and worthy of our obedience. That is, the first part
of the originalist exercise is to determine what the Constitution actually
means. Only then can we decide whether what it says is good. It may be
that once we interpret the Constitution – once we discover its meaning – we decide that it's a bad constitution and should be abandoned.

There are generally two theories of why we should be originalists
as a matter of interpretation, independent of whether the Constitution
is legitimate. The first theory relies on the writtenness of the Constitution. The second relies on the nature of language, whether written
or unwritten, and ultimately the legal effect our legal system accords
to the meaning of a law's words. Not all legal systems *must* accord
legal significance to a law's words, but ours surely does, and for good
reason: our system of laws has determined over its thousand-year
evolution that according meaning legal significance serves "rule of
law" values such as predictability, fairness, consistency, and stability.

I shall start by surveying two key originalists who make an argument
from writtenness – Randy Barnett and Keith Whittington – whose works
we shall also encounter later when we discuss various theories
of legitimacy. Barnett is a natural rights thinker, and Whittington is
a popular sovereignty thinker. Both rely on the writtenness of the

Constitution for their arguments about originalism. These arguments from writtenness are interesting and important, but I don't think writtenness proves we have to be originalist. That is so at least because nonoriginalists plausibly claim that written text can play a role without requiring originalism, and more convincingly, from my perspective, I'm not sure that having an *unwritten* constitution means a legal system should *not* be originalist.

I will instead suggest that the form of our fundamental law – that is, whether it be in a single written constitution, in a series of judicial opinions and legislative acts, as in the British "unwritten" constitution, or even in a series of oral communications – may perhaps determine the ease or difficulty of *changing* the existing content of the law. It affects what we will describe as a legal system's "secondary" rules of change, such as (in our case) the amendment process, but not its existing "primary" rules that govern our current behavior. Whether the constitution is written or unwritten should not affect how we interpret the law as it now stands; that is, our interpretation of the rules we look to *now* to govern our private behavior or official conduct should not vary depending on whether the constitution is written, unwritten, or oral.

I think the more persuasive argument for originalism thus depends on the nature of *all* communication. Whether a constitution (or any law) is written or unwritten – that is, whether it is written in a single fundamental document; in a long series of legislative acts and judicial opinions, as in England; or even in a series of oral communications – so long as its communicative content is known, we should give that content its original public meaning.

But we are getting ahead of ourselves – let us start with writtenness.

WRITTENNESS

Barnett writes that the "impetus" for interpreting the Constitution with its original meaning is the same as what drives our interpretation of any written contract. We often do not enforce oral contracts because we are unsure that the parties actually agreed to the alleged terms. (This rule comes from the old English statute of frauds, of which every U.S. state has some version today.) If a contract is written, we also don't usually accept outside, nonwritten evidence to elucidate its meaning. (This is called the "parol evidence rule."[2])

The reason we interpret everyday contracts this way is that *writing* serves certain important functions. According to Barnett (and others who have come before him), writing serves four key functions in particular: evidentiary, cautionary, channeling, and clarification. Writing is *evidence* that a certain transaction took place. Writing also serves a *cautionary* function by requiring an opportunity to "reflect and deliberate" on the wisdom of the agreement. It serves a *channeling* function by focusing the public's awareness on a given agreement for achieving a desired result. Finally, it serves a *clarification* function because writings are usually more detailed than oral agreements. Creating a written constitution is valuable for precisely these reasons, too.

Barnett also argues that our Constitution is intended to restrict or restrain lawmakers and other government officials, and that purpose would be subverted by allowing the meaning of those restraints to vary over time. Keith Whittington similarly argues that we have to be originalist because there was a perceived need in the revolutionary period to *fix* the principles of government in a *permanent* text, unlike Great Britain's unwritten constitution, and that writing down those principles makes them more judicially enforceable.[3] It certainly makes sense that if the principles of government are to be permanent, we ought to write them down and interpret the words through which they are expressed in an unchangeable way. It may be that having a written text is some evidence of a commitment to originalism.

But I'm not sure it proves we have to be originalist, for two reasons. On the one hand, many other countries have written constitutions that are interpreted in a nonoriginalist way, and even nonoriginalists believe the Constitution's text is relevant; they just argue it need not be given its original public meaning. They might say the text serves cautionary, evidentiary, and channeling functions, but that doesn't require originalism. For example, David Strauss argues that the right to have assistance of counsel for one's defense can plausibly mean the government should pay for your lawyer, even though that was not the original understanding, because at least it is consistent with a contemporary understanding of the text.[4] The text would still serve at least a cautionary, channeling, and clarification function, but it's not originalist.

More generally, all of the "settlement values" nonoriginalists claim as justifying some obedience to the Constitution – which we will explore in more depth in the final chapter – rely on the writtenness of the Constitution. It is a good thing the Constitution is written because, as Strauss and others might say, that increases stability and allows us to settle important questions (even if they aren't settled right). A written text can serve as the locus of a constitutional culture in which we debate its meaning in modern times. And so on.

Conversely, the other reason I think writtenness does not prove we have to be originalist is because it hardly follows that we should not be originalist otherwise. That is, we should not be *non*originalist merely because the fundamental law is communicated orally, or communicated in a series of written legislative acts and judicial opinions, as in England. One would think that the same "rule of law" values served by interpreting a written constitution with its original public meaning, and all the other values served by such writing, would equally justify adhering to the original public meaning of the fundamental law even when it is communicated orally or in more than a single constitutional document.

Rather, I think the critical difference among these different kinds of legal systems has to do with what H. L. A. Hart called "secondary rules of change."[5] The *primary* rules of a system are the legal prohibitions and injunctions that *currently* exist. These primary rules determine what you and I are allowed to do right now, as we speak. Our Constitution's primary rules determine what our government officials are allowed to do – for example, what types of legislation Congress is allowed to pass. But the legal system then has another class of legal rules: the "secondary rules" that affect the primary rules themselves. These rules do not tell us or our officials how to behave right now, but they determine things such as how the primary rules themselves are permitted to change. For example, the amendment process is our constitutional system's secondary rule of change.

I think writtenness can affect these secondary rules, but I don't think it has much to do with the primary rules – with what the current law *is*. In other words, in these other kinds of legal systems, it might be easier to *change* the law, for example, by issuing a new oral communication, important act of Parliament, or fundamental judicial opinion.

But that it is easier to change the law in these other systems does not affect the question of what the law *is* until such changes occur. Thus, a written constitution is consistent with the notion of fixing principles because it is harder to change the content of the law in a system with a written constitution than in a system with an unwritten constitution – at least if the written constitution, like ours, has a strict secondary rule of change. But that does not answer how we are to determine the content of the *current* law, i.e., the primary rules that actually govern private and official behavior now.

Put differently, I don't think a written constitution is necessarily evidence of a commitment to originalism. Rather, it is a commitment to the particular secondary rule of change written into the particular constitution, and, if that rule of change is very strict, such as in ours, it is also indirectly a commitment to the *particular primary rules that existed at the time the text was written.* That our written Constitution establishes a rule of change whose requirements are hard to meet (such as our amendment process) does at least indirectly demonstrate a commitment to the primary rules preferred by our Founders. These are the primary rules that tell Congress, the president, the courts, and the state governments what they can and cannot do. Having a written constitution with a burdensome secondary rule of change shows a commitment to the Founders and their principles, which are hard to change, but not to originalism as such.[6]

I think Barnett and Whittington get closest to providing the best reasons we should be originalists when they rely instead on the nature of language and human communication. Barnett explains, for example, that we interpret everyday contracts through their "objective" meaning:

> Because people cannot read each other's minds, they must rely on appearances when making their decision of whether to enter or to refrain from entering into a contractual relationship. Thus, in contract law, though we are concerned about the intentions of the parties, we are concerned about only those intentions the parties have succeeded in manifesting to each other, and not with any uncommunicated subjective intentions. We rely on the public or objective meaning of contractual terms because this is the meaning to which the parties have committed themselves. ... The same is true of constitutions.[7]

Barnett is onto something. Surely when parties communicate, they "are concerned about only those intentions the parties have succeeded in manifesting to each other." But writtenness might not be playing such a big role here. Writing something down surely helps us determine what has been agreed to, but in theory when people make *oral* agreements, they are also "concerned about ... those intentions the parties have" manifested to each other. Barnett intuits something that we will elaborate upon shortly: *any* communication intended for a public audience, as a default rule, is interpreted by its original public meaning. That's simply how language works. That's how you, the reader, are interpreting what I'm writing right now.

Whittington similarly argues:

> [C]ommunication assumes both commonality and intentionality by those attempting to communicate. ... If language is to communicate a meaning that meaning must not only be available to others but must also be available to others by means of the language used. Such meaning is available to others not because of some natural relationship between objects and words but because the meaning of words is defined through their intersubjective use. Language is not private, because meanings are not private. ... [M]eaning, or intention, is embedded in the language itself, is realized with the utterance.[8]

That makes a lot of sense: the ability to communicate implies shared, common understandings of the meanings of words. But notice that this has little to do with writtenness – Whittington is describing a feature of all language.

What we should take away is that there is *value* in writing down a constitution in a single fundamental document. When you write down the communicative content of a constitution, that serves evidentiary, cautionary, channeling, and clarification functions. And it may make it harder to *change* the current, "primary rules" of the system, depending on the secondary rule of change you write into the text. Thus, it is easier to fix principles. But it does not follow that having an oral constitution – or a constitution enshrined in more than one fundamental written document – suggests that we do *not* have to be originalist.

I believe we have to be originalist no matter how the law is communicated. The written nature of the Constitution serves important values, especially as they concern a legal system's rules of change. But the argument for interpreting any system's *current* (or primary) rules as originalists is much more fundamental and simple: we must be originalists because *any* communication, whether written or oral – and particularly if it is intended for a public audience – is always interpreted by its original public meaning unless we have some indication that the communication was intended to be interpreted in some other way. And our understanding of "rule of law" requires that we live by those public meanings. Let's try to see why.

ON FRIED-CHICKEN RECIPES AND CONSTITUTIONS

The proposition we are investigating is whether the original public meaning is *the* meaning of any public communication, and whether our legal system gives legal effect to such meaning. Let us start with what Jack Balkin has written about why he claims to be an originalist. Balkin is a progressive who has adopted the label originalism for his own theory of constitutional interpretation. We shall discuss his theory in more depth in the coming chapters. The important point for now is that even a progressive constitutional thinker can see the obviousness of this proposition about the nature of language. As he has written, to maintain the framework of the Constitution over time, "we must preserve the meaning of the words that constitute the framework."[9] He says elsewhere: "If we do not attempt to preserve legal meaning over time, then we will not be following the written Constitution as our plan but instead will be following a different plan."[10]

Isn't that obvious? What is the Constitution *but* the meaning of its words? Note that Balkin's point does not depend on the written nature of the Constitution. Although he mentions "written Constitution" in the second quotation, he could just as easily have taken that out: "If we do not attempt to preserve legal meaning over time, then we will not be following the Constitution as our plan but instead will be following a different plan." This point is so self-evident that, as one legal scholar has written, it takes an advanced degree to obscure it.

But what exactly is the meaning of "meaning"? Why do we focus on the *original public meaning* of the text instead of the contemporary public meaning, or an original secret meaning? Let us tackle the first proposition: we must look at original rather than contemporary meaning.

The answer is that the content of all communication is fixed at the time of its utterance. Law professor Larry Solum writes frequently on this topic and provides two examples to demonstrate this proposition. Let us take the example of a letter written in the twelfth century that uses the term *deer*. Today, this word refers to a very specific animal. As Solum explains, a deer refers to "a ruminant mammal belonging to the family Cervidae" and to a "number of broadly similar animals from related families within the order Artiodactyla." But it wasn't always so. In Middle English, the word *deer* meant a beast or animal of *any* kind.

Therefore, "One can only understand an ordinary letter written between 1066 and the fifteenth century that employed the term 'deer' by looking to the term's conventional semantic meaning at the time of writing; reading the letter and understanding the term 'deer' to refer exclusively to a mammal belonging to the family Cervidae would be a type of factual error – a linguistic mistake."[11] To interpret it any other way would be to misconstrue reality. And the semantic content does not depend on the writing: even an oral communication using *deer* would have the meaning given by ordinary usage in Middle English.

Solum points to an interesting possible example of this kind of semantic drift in the U.S. Constitution. Article IV, Section 4 states that the United States shall protect every state in the union "against domestic Violence." The contemporary semantic meaning of the phrase "domestic violence," Solum notes, is "intimate partner abuse," "battering," or "wife-beating"; it is the "physical, sexual, psychological, and economic abuse that takes place in the context of an intimate relationship, including marriage." Yet the Framers meant "insurrection" or "rebellion."

It would be a "linguistic mistake," a plain-and-simple factual error, to interpret this clause of the Constitution as referring to the modern kind of "domestic violence." We must interpret the words as they were originally understood because their very meaning is fixed at the time of their utterance. There is no getting around it: "[T]he phrase is understood as referring to its meaning at the time of origin, which encompasses the period roughly contemporaneous with the Framing and ratification – or formal legal approval – of the particular clause or amendment."[12]

We see now why it would be erroneous to interpret any communication, whether oral or written, with a contemporary semantic meaning that has drifted from the semantic meaning at the time of utterance. Such an interpretation would be a linguistic mistake. But moreover, to permit contemporary public meaning to supply our rules of law would be to give *random, accidental drifts* in language an *authority* to determine the law. Yet no theory of political philosophy of which I am aware would justify accidental and random semantic drift as a legal system's secondary rule of change.

Although it seems rather obvious that we must also look to the original *public* meaning, it is helpful to think through that proposition as well. To do so, we'll take a look at a rather entertaining law review article called "On Reading Recipes ... and Constitutions" by law professor Gary Lawson.[13] In this article, Lawson compares reading a constitution to reading a recipe for fried chicken. "Suppose," writes Lawson, "that we find a document hidden in an old house." This document

> appears to be written in English, and both linguistic analysis and scientific dating techniques indicate that the document was produced in the late-eighteenth century in the area commonly known as Philadelphia, Pennsylvania. The document lists quantities of items such as "one 2 1/2 pound chicken," "1/4 cup of flour," "one teaspoon of salt," "plenty of lard for frying," and "pepper to taste." It also contains instructions for combining and manipulating those items, such as "combine the one teaspoon of salt with the 1/4 cup of flour," "add pepper to taste to the salt and flour mixture," "coat the chicken with the flour," and "fry the coated chicken in hot lard until golden brown." The document, in other words, appears to be a late-eighteenth-century recipe for preparing fried chicken.

Now, Lawson only half jokes when he writes, "Sophisticated academics, however, find this document to be a great puzzle. After all, we cannot really *know* that it is a recipe, can we? Perhaps it was a secret code giving instructions to military troops. Perhaps it was a private diary," and so on. But really, of course the document is a recipe: "any fool can see that"!

So what does the recipe mean? Lawson explains that we know, from our general knowledge of recipes, that recipes are "sets of instructions designed to achieve specific goals" and that they are intended to be read by persons other than the author. "Such recipes present themselves to the world of human observers as communications of a particular kind," and accordingly, the meaning of a recipe is its *public* meaning – "the meaning that it would have to the audience to which the document addresses itself."

That makes sense. A recipe would be poor indeed if it were written in code. The idea is for others to read it and understand the meaning its author intended to convey. And because every document is created "at a particular moment in space and time, documents ordinarily ... speak to an audience at the time of their creation and draw their meaning from that point." Because the recipe presents itself to the world as a public document, its meaning "is its original public meaning."

That doesn't mean the document won't be ambiguous, or that there won't be interpretive problems. Adding pepper to "taste" is not very specific. Whose taste are we talking about? And won't that vary from person to person? Does "flour" refer to any powdered grain product or to a specific one? But these questions have to do with *how* to apply rather than *whether* to apply a methodology of original public meaning. We still interpret the recipe with its original public meaning.

Now, let us suppose that over the centuries, cooks began to make fried chicken in different ways. Suppose they now substitute rosemary for pepper because that seems to be what contemporary fried-chicken eaters prefer. Does this modern practice affect the meaning of the recipe? Clearly not: "The recipe says 'pepper,' and if modern cooks use rosemary instead, they are not *interpreting* the original recipe, but rather they are *amending* it – perhaps for the better, but amending it nonetheless. The term 'pepper' is simply not ambiguous in this respect."

The change over time raises a different inquiry entirely: Should we still follow the old recipe? Maybe we decide that it's just not a good recipe for fried chicken. It got the most basic ingredient wrong. Perhaps the recipe no longer deserves our obedience today because people just don't like pepper anymore. But that doesn't change what the recipe *means*. Its meaning is fixed in time.

So what is different about reading a constitution? Absolutely nothing. A constitution is but a recipe for government. Lawson concludes:

"As a recipe of sorts that is clearly addressed to an external audience, the Constitution's meaning is its original public meaning. Other approaches to interpretation are simply wrong. Interpreting the Constitution is no more difficult, and no different in principle, than interpreting a late-eighteenth-century recipe for fried chicken."

I once heard the objection, however, that not all language is necessarily interpreted by its original public meaning; for example, novels often leave room for multiple interpretations, the reader's own perspective, and so on. The first point to make is that the Constitution, well, isn't a novel. It is not a poem or a Socratic dialogue intended to be read ironically, nor is it a set of secret instructions to the Illuminati. It is, like the fried-chicken recipe, a set of *public* instructions for a *public* audience, with the intent of guiding the behavior of those it governs. It is, in this respect, like all laws and most other legal instruments.

But it's also worth pointing out that even when it is a novel we are expounding (to adapt Chief Justice John Marshall's famous phrase), that doesn't mean all interpretations are created equal. Words may be used in such a way that they produce different effects on different readers. They can be used to create ambiguity. Some words create ambiguity without their author having intended to create ambiguity at all. No originalist disputes that the Constitution is sometimes, like a novel, hard to interpret. No one disputes that different readers – even at the time of the Founding – might have or have had different understandings of the text. The point is only that each word still has a standard, objective, and public meaning; that conventional usage limits what we can do with the words; and some interpretations are better than others.

Most of us can now comfortably conclude that we cannot but interpret the Constitution through a method of original public meaning. The Constitution was addressed to a public audience at a certain time, and its meaning was fixed at that time. The question of whether the Constitution is legitimate is entirely separate. Perhaps we don't think we should keep following it today. In that case, we can either amend the Constitution or perhaps openly revolt – or do something in between, like have a new constitutional convention.

THE LEGAL EFFECT OF ORIGINAL MEANING

Some nonoriginalists, however, will raise the same objections against writtenness in this context as well. They'll say that the original public meaning of the text is certainly *one* source of constitutional law. It is surely at least something we look at to decide what a particular legal ruling should be. These nonoriginalists don't want to ignore it completely. But neither does starting with the text mean that original public meaning exhausts the tools at our disposal, they'll say. For example, one nonoriginalist, Andrew Coan, has written that the "text of the Constitution" has "an important role,"

> but what exactly [nonoriginalism] understands "the text" to mean requires more explanation. The short answer is that the text refers to the full range of meanings present-day Americans might plausibly understand its written words to convey, including but not limited to original public meaning, the intended meaning of the Framers and Ratifiers, contemporary public meaning, and glosses attached to the text by history and tradition.[14]

Kent Greenawalt similarly argues that "a satisfactory account of how judges should resolve constitutional cases must be irreducibly pluralist," that is, "[o]ver a range of cases, judges need to take into account a variety of factors in reaching decisions."[15]

A sensible originalist would hardly disagree that sometimes – perhaps many times – original meaning doesn't fully resolve a constitutional question (see more on this in Chapter 5), and that precedent, institutional considerations, and perhaps even extraconstitutional factors might sometimes bear on the question at hand. But what does a nonoriginalist do in cases of *contradiction* – when the original meaning says *x*, but his nonoriginalist interpretation says *not x*? Let us assume that the meaning of the Commerce Clause did not encompass the kind of broad federal powers permitted by the Supreme Court of the last eighty years or so. We may think it better that the federal government have these powers, but we shouldn't kid ourselves either – if we grant the government these powers, we have effectively amended our recipe for government. We have amended the Constitution through Supreme Court decisions and public acquiescence. Does that mean the words of the Commerce Clause *mean* that the federal government has all these powers? No. The words' meaning is fixed. We've just decided to ignore that meaning. Nonoriginalists have yet to come up with a satisfactory explanation for displacing clear original meaning with something contradictory other than that it might lead to more desirable results according to their own conceptions of good policy.[16]

Of course, as an *originalist* matter, our legal system sometimes has rules that allow us to override otherwise clear statutory meaning, and the previous chapter noted the example of the absurdity doctrine. Recall also from that discussion that meaning doesn't always determine the entire legal effect of a law. In our killing prohibition, we had to consider other rules in the legal system about self-defense, conspiracy, and so on, even if the text of the statute at hand was silent on those matters.[17] But that doesn't mean we are ignoring the law – it merely means we are situating it among the other preexisting legal rules in the system. The Constitution may have an original public meaning, but that doesn't necessarily tell us what the *legal effect* of that meaning should be.

What nonoriginalists seek is to undermine the legal effect of original meaning beyond what the existing legal rules of the system already permit. As I noted in the Introduction, a legal system does not *have* to be the way our system is. For example, we could have a legal system in which the meaning of the words isn't binding or in which the legal effect of the words departs significantly from original meaning. We could have a system in which all statutes are intended merely to guide the discretion of judges, who are required to do "justice" in any case that comes before them. But this is not how we interpret laws. It's just not *our* legal system.

And there are entirely good reasons why that isn't our system: over the thousand or so years in which English and American law has developed, our system has concluded that the very concept of "rule of law" requires giving legal effect to the meaning of the words of a law. Predictability, fairness, consistency, and stability values are served by treating the meaning of the words as authoritative – or at least paramount. Put another way, we surely have to justify normatively why we *ought* to give legal effect to the ordinary, public meaning of laws – and these are the values that justify doing so. Would we rather be governed by judges who use the words of statutes merely as "guides" to their otherwise unbridled discretion? The reason, then, we don't interpret any other written law as Coan desires to interpret the Constitution is because it violates our system's very understanding of the rule of law. This may explain why our legal system appears to be originalist as a matter of our actual legal practices.[18]

Once we accept that this is the way laws are interpreted in our legal system, there are only two conceivable reasons why we should interpret a constitution in a different way. The first is that we think the Constitution *should* say something other than what it says, and should establish a constitutional regime other than the one it in fact establishes. That goes to the question of legitimacy and whether we should obey the Constitution in the first place. It has nothing to do with what the Constitution says or the constitutional order it creates. The second claim nonoriginalists can make is that our *legal system* should change; they might claim that we should not give paramount legal effect to a law's words. But that, surely, is a much harder argument to make, and one that nonoriginalists usually don't.

In sum, nonoriginalists cannot justify why the original public meaning can be overridden by other interpretive tools. All the arguments to give precedence to other interpretive elements, to other tools, are merely arguments for ignoring the *law* – the communicative content of the commands given, whether those commands be oral or written. We might think the Constitution with all of its modern glosses is a better Constitution. So be it; but let's not pretend that those glosses are what the words actually mean. We might, finally, think that our entire legal system should be changed so as not to give authoritative or paramount importance to the meaning of words in giving legal effect to the laws. But anyone making *that* argument has quite the hill to climb.

THE CONSTITUTION CAN STILL ADAPT TO CHANGING CIRCUMSTANCES

There is usually one final hiccup. Someone usually asks: Does originalism mean the Constitution can't adapt to future circumstances? Does it mean we are stuck with a woefully outdated document? Let me put the inquiry more concretely. If the framers and ratifiers of the Fourteenth Amendment did not believe it required desegregating schools, does that mean *Brown v. Board* was wrongly decided? Does that mean we're stuck with segregation? What about the Eighth Amendment? Does the phrase "cruel and unusual" punishment necessarily prohibit only those punishments that would have been considered cruel and unusual in 1789?

Those are tricky examples. But the general answer is simple: no. If it were true that originalists believed that only the original expected *applications* of the Constitution are valid, then the First Amendment would not apply to speech on the Internet. Then the Fourth Amendment's guarantee against unreasonable searches and seizures would not apply to GPS devices. And so on. The simple answer is that most of the provisions of the Constitution define certain standards or principles – unreasonable searches and seizures, equal protection, due process – that have certain meanings that can apply to new situations. How the framers of a particular constitutional provision expected that provision to be applied is certainly evidence of original meaning, but that is not the same thing as saying only the originally expected applications are valid.[19]

In a more technical jargon from the philosophy of language, we might say that the words of the Constitution have a certain *sense* – they express a certain function – and we apply this sense, or this function, to facts and conditions to get certain results. There are different ways to refer to the result of the function, but we may loosely describe it as the "referent" of the words.

Here is an example to illustrate what I mean by this, which I borrow from a law review article on originalism and this sense-reference distinction.[20] Suppose you have a fork on the northeast corner of a table and a fork on the southwest corner. If someone were to say, "Remove all forks on the northern edge of the table," you'd remove the fork in the northeast corner. But if someone were to say, "Remove all forks on the eastern edge of the table," you'd remove the same fork. The *referent* of the expressions is the same – the fork in the northeast corner. But clearly the *sense* of each expression is different. The *eastern* edge is not the same thing as the *northern* edge.

The gist is that a smart originalist will normally understand that the provisions of the Constitution enshrine a *sense* that does not change with time. But the facts and conditions to which the sense applies – the *referents* of the constitutional provisions – can change. Now, sometimes originalists fail to see the distinction clearly. Justice Scalia did, alas, frequently assume that the Eighth Amendment's prohibition on cruel and unusual punishments only applies to those punishments considered cruel and unusual in 1789. But that need not necessarily be the case. (In any event, Justice Scalia's shortcoming in this respect seemed limited to the Eighth Amendment and perhaps the Due Process Clause.)

Although we will not get into it now, the sense-reference distinction, or the distinction between meaning and application, is at least one way to justify the result in *Brown v. Board of Education*. We shall take that up in Chapter 7.

WERE THE FOUNDERS ORIGINALISTS?

What if the Founders were not originalist? What if the original interpretive conventions the Founders used, or expected the future to use, were nonoriginalist tools of interpretation? Then an originalist would have to be nonoriginalist. Recall that this is the attack H. Jefferson Powell made in his 1985 article, which we briefly discussed in the previous chapter. He argued that the Founders did not intend for their intentions to govern, and therefore originalism is self-defeating.

But Powell's attack applies only to original *intentions* originalism, as we have also discussed. It does not follow that the Founders would not have adopted the original public meaning of the Constitution's words. To ask now whether the Founders were originalist is the same as to ask, "Did the Founders interpret the text of the Constitution as they would have interpreted other legal texts, other written texts, and any human communication intended for a public audience for that matter?" Even a guess here will do: of course the Founders were originalists in this sense. They thought words had their ordinary, public meanings.

Powell in his own article confirms as much. He writes: "The Philadelphia framers' primary expectation regarding constitutional interpretation was that the Constitution, like any other legal document, would be interpreted in accord with its express language."[21] He goes

on to say: "The framers shared the traditional common law view ...
that the import of the document they were framing would be determined by reference to the intrinsic meaning of its words or through the
usual judicial process of case-by-case interpretation."[22]

That's exactly the kind of "original public meaning" originalism we
have been describing. Powell cites broadly from the founding generation to show that they understood that a legal instrument would be
interpreted by the public meaning of the words as clarified by conventions of usage. More recent historical and legal scholarship confirms
this. Caleb Nelson quotes from several of James Madison's letters from
the 1820s and 1830s:

> "In the exposition of laws, and even of Constitutions," [Madison]
> exclaimed, "how many important errors may be produced by mere
> innovations in the use of words and phrases, if not controulable
> by a recurrence to the *original and authentic meaning* attached
> to them!" Other letters from Madison reflect the same view: "The
> change which the meaning of words inadvertently undergoes" is a
> source of "misconstructions of the Constitutional text," and it
> would be "preposterous" to let "the effect of time in changing the
> meaning of words and phrases" justify "new constructions" of
> written constitutions and laws.[23]

In an 1824 letter Madison wrote, "What a metamorphosis would be
produced in the code of law if all its ancient phraseology were to be
taken in its modern sense."[24]

There can be no doubt, in light of letters such as these, that James
Madison was what we would today call an originalist. Indeed, the
Founders sought original meaning when interpreting all laws and
treaties too. Vattel's 1758 treatise on the law of nations, which
"enjoyed canonical status among Americans of the founding generation,"[25] declared that because "[l]anguages are constantly varying in
form" and "the force and meaning of terms change in the course of
time," when we "interpret a very old treaty we must know the common
use of the terms at the time the treaty was drawn up."[26] An influential
treatise on statutory interpretation explained that because "[l]aws
operate at a distance of time," subsequent interpreters must look
"back" to "contemporary [original] practice" to "see in what sense
it was then understood."[27] And as David Currie explains in his

monumental study of constitutional interpretation in Congress between 1789 and 1861, even in the Jacksonian era – a generation or two removed from the Founding itself – "just about everybody was an originalist."[28]

It is of course *possible* the Framers would not have thought the words should have their original public meaning. We have said that original public meaning is a *default* rule for all communication intended for a public audience. But surely we cannot interpret the Constitution by any secret meaning. The Constitution addresses itself to a public audience, and even if we had some way of knowing what its secret meaning was, what would give that secret meaning any legitimacy? It may be that the Founders expected the words to drift – but Madison's letters put that notion to bed. None of this is to say that the Founders did not think our Constitution would have to adapt to changing circumstances. They all understood that it would have to be applied in new situations. But they all understood that the sense and meaning of the words of the Constitution were fixed in time (or, in some instances, would become fixed over time), even if some ambiguity or uncertainty remained about just how those words would play out in the real world.

CONCLUSION: *FEDERALIST* NO. 37

I would like to conclude with the following passages from *Federalist* No. 37, which, in my view, is perhaps the most elegant of all the *Federalist Papers*. In that number, James Madison describes both the power and the limitations of human language and the human mind, and how those limitations affect the enterprise of writing and interpreting a constitution. I shall quote it at length:

> The faculties of the mind itself have never yet been distinguished and defined with satisfactory precision by all the efforts of the most acute and metaphysical philosophers. Sense, perception, judgment, desire, volition, memory, imagination are found to be separated by such delicate shades and minute gradations that their boundaries have eluded the most subtle investigations, and remain a pregnant source of ingenious disquisition and controversy....

All new laws, though penned with the greatest technical skill, and passed on the fullest and most mature deliberation, are considered as more or less obscure and equivocal, until their meaning be liquidated and ascertained by a series of particular discussions and adjudications. Besides the obscurity arising from the complexity of objects, and the imperfection of the human faculties, the medium through which the conceptions of men are conveyed to each other adds a fresh embarrassment. The use of words is to express ideas. Perspicuity, therefore, requires not only that the ideas should be distinctly formed, but that they should be expressed by words distinctly and exclusively appropriate to them. But no language is so copious as to supply words and phrases for every complex idea, or so correct as not to include many equivocally denoting different ideas. Hence it must happen that however accurately objects may be discriminated in themselves, and however accurately the discrimination may be considered, the definition of them may be rendered inaccurate by the inaccuracy of the terms in which it is delivered. And this unavoidable inaccuracy must be greater or less, according to the complexity and novelty of the objects defined. When the Almighty himself condescends to address mankind in their own language, his meaning, luminous as it must be, is rendered dim and doubtful by the cloudy medium through which it is communicated.

Here, then, are three sources of vague and incorrect definitions: indistinctness of the object, imperfection of the organ of conception, inadequateness of the vehicle of ideas. Any one of these must produce a certain degree of obscurity. The convention, in delineating the boundary between the federal and State jurisdictions, must have experienced the full effect of them all.[29]

What can we take away from this wonderful passage? First, all natural human communication will necessarily be somewhat obscure and indeterminate. That will be particularly true when we are dealing with a constitution that advances an altogether new theory of government, with complex ideas for which existing words may be unable to cope. But we also learn, secondly, that the words are used to express ideas, and these ideas are fixed at the time of the writing or utterance. Words may imperfectly express the ideas, but ideas they still express.

Third and lastly, we learn what might be done in the event of obscurity, ambiguity, and indeterminacy. Madison explains that "[a]ll new laws, though penned with the greatest technical skill, and passed on the fullest and most mature deliberation, are considered as more or less obscure and equivocal, until their meaning be liquidated and ascertained by a series of particular discussions and adjudications." This is his theory of "liquidation," which we shall encounter again in Chapter 5. It is a way of resolving ambiguity. It may be that the words create some ambiguity, that the ideas expressed have uncertain applications. But over time those ambiguities will get resolved in favor of one interpretation or another; it is at that point, at that particular adjudication or discussion, that the meaning of the words can become fixed for future generations.

PART II

The Original Constitution

3 CONSTITUTIONAL LEGITIMACY

"That to secure these rights, Governments are instituted among Men, deriving their just powers from the consent of the governed."[1]

The Declaration of Independence (1776)

A TALE OF THREE THEORIES

In the previous chapter, we explored the idea that we must be originalists because the nature of language and our legal system requires it. We now address our second inquiry: Accepting that we have to be originalists, is the Constitution as originally understood a legitimate document worthy of our obedience? After all, we could conclude that we have to be originalists but that the Constitution is a bad constitution. In that case we would be justified in seeking constitutional amendments or, if the Constitution were extremely unjust, perhaps a revolution in government.

In this chapter we will explore what three prominent schools of originalism have to say about constitutional legitimacy.[2] These three schools – which we may loosely label as a libertarian school, a progressive-originalist school, and a conservative school – all claim that we have to be originalists because of the "writtenness" of the Constitution, or because of the nature of language in our legal system. But whether we ought to obey the Constitution is another matter entirely – and libertarian, progressive, and conservative originalists all offer different answers.

Libertarian originalists argue that the Constitution must protect natural rights to be legitimate. When properly understood through an originalist lens, the Constitution does, they argue, protect natural rights, although modern interpretations protect these rights far less today. Progressive originalists argue that the Constitution must allow for responsiveness to contemporary politics to be legitimate, and that the Constitution does indeed allow for such responsiveness in its broad and grand provisions such as the Due Process Clause and the Equal Protection Clause. Conservative originalists argue that the Constitution is legitimate because it was rooted in an act of popular sovereignty when the people ratified the Constitution in 1789 in the various state conventions established for that purpose.

THE LIBERTARIAN THEORY: NATURAL RIGHTS

The libertarian theory offers a justification for constitutional obedience under conditions in which our natural rights are protected. We will therefore explore this theory's understanding of natural rights: What do they entail? Where do they come from? In so doing, we will become somewhat acquainted with the thinking of natural rights theorists. In Chapter 4 we will see that the Founders did share many of these natural rights views, but that natural rights were not the only component of their thinking.

Randy Barnett, one of the most prominent natural-rights constitutional thinkers in the legal academy, makes the case in his book *Restoring the Lost Constitution: The Presumption of Liberty* that the Constitution must protect natural rights for it to be just and worthy of our obedience today. He argues that popular sovereignty is an inadequate basis for constitutional obedience: only a constitution that "contains adequate procedures" to protect natural rights can lay a claim to legitimacy and our obedience.[3] A constitution that lacks procedures to protect natural rights "is illegitimate even if it was consented to by a majority."[4]

He first takes on the validity of several consent-based arguments for constitutional obedience. Most people today instinctively (and I think correctly) believe that the Constitution is at least partly legitimate because it was enacted by "We the People." But Barnett calls this "We the People" a fiction. Surely we don't "consent" when we vote for the guy who loses. And what about those who abstain from voting altogether? Doesn't consenting imply that there is some way we can withhold consent? And how can we do that? Moreover, no such thing as "tacit" consent arises merely from our choice to reside in this country because that assumes those in power have the authority in the first place to tell us to obey or to leave. Nor could the Founders consent for us, because the same problems with consent apply to them, not to mention that their consent took place long ago.

In short, that the Constitution was ratified by popular assemblies in the late 1780s makes no difference; indeed, it appears that even if the Constitution were formally abolished today and re-ratified with exactly the same text, then, assuming it was not just by Barnett's conception, it would not provide any better reason for non-consenting parties to adhere to its commands.

We won't stop here to assess the merits of his attack on popular sovereignty. We shall see later in this chapter the arguments in favor of a popular sovereignty theory of obedience. We are now interested merely in identifying the problems natural-rights thinkers associate with popular sovereignty and why they think the protection of natural rights is a better foundation for constitutional legitimacy.

So why must a constitution protect natural rights instead? Barnett puts it this way. Consider a society of a few hundred people. It would be possible to achieve unanimous consent in such a society. In that society, the people could choose to infringe on "natural rights" as much as they wanted. If every single person agreed to restrict freedom, why would anyone be justified in disobeying? Everyone voted in favor.

But we don't live in such a society; no such society exists on the face of the earth (or ever existed). All modern political communities are too large to achieve unanimous consent. So why should I obey any command if I don't personally agree to it? Barnett's answer is that so long as this command does not violate any preexisting right that I have, then I am obliged to obey it. Put inversely, any command that *does* violate my rights, so long as I did not consent to it, I would not have to obey. That makes a lot of sense.

But just what are these preexisting rights? Anyone could always *claim* that such-and-such is a "right" and that therefore the government can't take it away. How do we know just what rights have to be protected for the Constitution to be just and worthy of our obedience? That is a key argument against a natural-rights theory of legitimacy: people disagree about what natural rights are. Libertarians claim that economic freedom is a natural right. They say the government violates our natural rights when it restricts our freedom to contract to, say, a twelve-hour workday in a manual-labor occupation, or to sub-minimum-wage work. Yet our government makes such restrictions all the time.

Progressives might say we have a natural right to abortion or to gay marriage. Consider the brief submitted by California Attorney General Jerry Brown when Proposition 8 – the California ballot proposition defining marriage to be between a man and a woman – was litigated in the courts. In it he wrote that the rights recognized as "inalienable" by the Framers of the Constitution "antedate" the constitution and are "inherent in human nature" – so far so good. But then he claimed that gay marriage is just such a right inherent in human nature. Now, I strongly favor gay marriage, and even believe we can progress in our understanding of what rights are natural and inalienable, but it is at least striking that this right was never conceived of before recent history to be a natural, rather than merely political, right.

Judge Alex Kozinski of the U.S. Court of Appeals for the Ninth Circuit in California, who is known as something of a libertarian firebrand, recently emphasized this problem with a natural-rights theory of the Constitution. "We also must realize," he wrote, "that the idea of what those natural rights are has changed, and will continue to change, over time."[5] He cites same-sex marriage as an example. And then he describes the arguments for and against considering abortion a natural right. Perhaps, as Amherst Professor Hadley Arkes argues, natural reasoning leads us to conclude that a fetus is a person. But, responds Kozinski, if a person attacks you, don't you have the right for self-preservation? Natural-rights arguments can often be cited both for and against a given right being a "natural" right.

But let's take a step back. That people disagree over the *content* of natural rights does not mean that natural rights do not exist. I am reminded of this wonderful passage from Allan Bloom's *The Closing of the American Mind*:

> [T]he fact that there have been different opinions about good and bad in different times and places in no way proves that none is true or superior to others. To say that it does so prove is as absurd as to say that the diversity of points of view expressed in a college bull session proves there is no truth. On the face of it, the difference of opinion would seem to raise the question as to which is true or right rather than to banish it.[6]

That's not to say that the pursuit of truth is necessarily easy. Quite the opposite. The pursuit of truth has tangled the minds of the greatest political philosophers of the Western and other traditions since at least what Karl Jaspers described as the Axial Age. This was the era of Confucius in China, Buddha in India, Zoroaster in Persia, Jeremiah in the Near East, and various Greek thinkers and writers – Homer, Thucydides, Sophocles, Socrates – and a time in which different modes of life were being propounded as examples of the good life.

Consider also that there is widespread, perhaps universal, agreement that some rights absolutely have to be protected. Although it was not a unanimous view at the time of the Founding, today most agree with James Madison, George Washington, and Thomas Jefferson that slavery is an abomination. If the Constitution today condoned or permitted slavery, no one would hesitate to charge it with injustice. It would be grounds for open rebellion. Now that we have settled on at least *one* right that must be protected, surely it is simply a matter of finding other rights that ought to be protected? Perhaps few rights command such universal approbation as the right to be free from slavery, but we ought to be open to arguments that there are others.

I will not attempt here to establish what these other rights are. Rather, I would like to suggest how one might go about investigating what they are. That investigation is what a traditional liberal arts education has engaged in for hundreds of years and what political philosophy has engaged in at least since Socrates' admonition that the unexamined life is not worth living. If we are to decide for ourselves whether natural rights exist and, if so, that the Constitution must therefore protect them, we need some way of thinking about what these natural rights are.

Let us begin with Barnett's understanding of natural rights, which he claims the Founders shared. Barnett essentially argues that natural rights are a form of liberty. As evidence that the Founders viewed them as such, he presents the Founders' enumerations of what they called "retained" rights. Roger Sherman, for example, explained that some of the rights retained by the people "are the rights of Conscience in matters of religion; of acquiring property, and of pursuing happiness & Safety; of Speaking, writing and publishing their Sentiments with decency and freedom; of peaceably assembling to consult their common good, and of applying to Government by petition or remonstrance for redress of grievances."[7] These rights, explains Barnett, "are liberties or freedoms to believe or act in certain ways" and are not "positive claims on government or on others." In sum, Barnett argues: "[N]atural rights define a private domain within which persons may do as they please, provided their conduct does not encroach upon the rightful domain of others."[8]

For those familiar with the history of political philosophy, that is similar to John Stuart Mill's famous "harm principle": the law should only coerce individuals when their actions might otherwise harm others. I am not so sure the Founders shared this view, but they certainly lived in the era of John Locke and modern natural rights. Locke argued that men are free and equal in the state of nature before we enter civil society.[9] Men have different talents and capabilities, but these are differences in degree and not in kind. We must enter civil society because there are many disadvantages to the state of nature: every man is a judge in his own cause and has the ability to harm others, and therefore the state of nature is not very safe or secure. We thus enter civil society to eliminate those disadvantages – but we do *not* enter civil society if it eliminates our basic freedom and equality. If in the state of nature we are all free and equal, why would anyone possibly give up this freedom and equality and put all power in the hands of, say, an arbitrary tyrant? No – we enter civil society only if we get the benefit of the bargain. We have certain rights and advantages by nature, and we enter civil society to *secure* those rights while diminishing the disadvantages of the state of nature.

Richard Epstein, perhaps the other most prominent libertarian thinker among constitutional scholars, makes this very point in justifying constitutional obedience. He begins, like Barnett, with abandoning consent as the justification for obedience to the state. Even tacit consent "becomes the thin edge of the wedge that grants legislators the lion's share of the surplus that Lockean institutions wish to keep out of their hands."[10] Tacit consent turns out to be a raw deal. To make the natural-rights, Lockean conception of the state viable, obligation cannot come from consent but must come instead from a theory of exchange between the sovereign and the individual in which both benefit:

> The bulwark of the individual is ... [now] that whenever any portion of [his property] is taken from him, he must receive from the state ... some equivalent or greater benefit as part of the same transaction. The categorical command that property shall not be taken without tacit consent [the Lockean theory] must therefore be rewritten to provide that property may be taken upon provision of just compensation.[11]

In other words, to be just, the Constitution must protect natural rights: we are by nature free and equal before entering civil society, we have certain rights and property, and so civil society must ensure that those rights are secured; and any necessary infringement on rights must come with a just compensation. Both Epstein and Barnett, then, argue that for the Constitution to be legitimate, it must protect natural rights. They abandon any notion of the consent of the governed as legitimating constitutional obedience.

Permit me now an aside. Because we are exploring how one might go about investigating natural rights, I should like to point out that neither the harm principle nor the natural-rights position is self-evidently true, nor are Lockean institutions self-evidently the best (though I suspect they are). The ancients had a different view.* They concluded that a life of virtue – rather than a life of liberty – led to happiness. They arrived at this conclusion through a concept of

---

* By "ancients" I loosely mean those in the tradition of Socrates, Plato, Aristotle, and their followers.

natural *law* (rather than natural *right*), the notion that there exists a moral order in nature that we can discern with our unassisted reason. We discern the moral order from the nature of things, from their unique functions. What is man's nature? What, to put it differently, makes man different from the beasts? Speech and reason do, and both presuppose a society. Reason and philosophy presuppose different points of view, i.e., that there are others to philosophize with. We are, in other words, social animals. What kind of moral law follows from this nature? The ancients concluded that the best, happiest human type is the one that fulfills man's unique function the most. That might be the political philosopher engaging his reasoning faculties or perhaps the gentleman exercising social virtues.

So doesn't nature demand that we have a regime – a constitutional government – that encourages virtue? Aristotle, for example, concluded that the best regime is the one in which men both rule and are ruled in turn. The regime that conduces most to human flourishing and happiness is the one in which all men participate in politics. It is a regime of self-government. Other ancient societies sought to cultivate other kinds of virtues: military virtue or religious virtue, for instance. But all of these aims are different from natural *right*, which claims that I have a freedom to act in a certain way without government infringing on that right. Isaiah Berlin famously described the distinction as that between "positive" and "negative" liberty.

It is not self-evident that a people under a regime of negative liberty will be the happiest. For example, it might be shown that a society that permits drug use, gambling, and prostitution does not produce happy citizens (though I suspect prohibiting these activities would often do far more harm than good). The point is only that, if to be happy we must rather act in those ways that make us fully human – by engaging in positive liberty and the social virtues – then would not a just regime have to create the conditions for such virtue? I think the Founders believed that although the regime they created was principally aimed at protecting liberty, it would also create the conditions in which such virtue could flourish.

For our purposes it is sufficient to understand how we might think about natural rights and whence the views of libertarian originalists derive. We cannot say at this point whether the right to bear arms, or the right to pursue an economic occupation without interference from government, is a natural right. The Founders did seem to think they were. But the important point is that although people might disagree over the content of natural rights, it is possible to reason about human nature – either from the natural law or natural rights perspective – to try to come up with answers. If we indeed believe that we are by nature free and equal and have many rights in the state of nature, then civil society must protect those rights. And so must the Constitution, if we are to obey it today.

THE PROGRESSIVE THEORY: CONTEMPORARY RESPONSIVENESS

We now come to the theory of progressive originalism. Many readers will rightly ask: How is this different from nonoriginalism? Indeed, perhaps it's not much different. But the chief proponent of progressive originalism, Jack Balkin, claims that his method is originalist. So we should tackle his claims head on, on his own terms. And, I think, there is some truth to his claims.

Jack Balkin attempted something of a coup with his book *Living Originalism*. He tried to appropriate originalism for progressive ends. He argues that if one properly understands the Framers' intent and also the language and structure of the Constitution, then an originalist understanding of the Constitution leads to living constitutionalism. To Balkin, a living constitutionalist is the true originalist. His fundamental argument is that the Constitution is written in three separate kinds of clauses – rules, standards, and principles – and that while constitutional rules are fixed (such as the requirement that the president be at least thirty-five years of age), the Framers left the text's standards and especially its principles to be fleshed out by future generations.[12]

Justice Scalia famously explained that the Constitution was intended to constrain the American people to avoid the "rotting" of our society and politics.[13] Balkin argues just the opposite. He claims the Framers intended the Constitution to enable future generations to put their own glosses on the Constitution rather than to constrain them. Now we must be careful to avoid a false dichotomy. Surely the

Constitution does a little of both: it enables us in some respects and constrains us in others. But Balkin emphasizes the enabling dimension far more than the constraining one.

Balkin avoids the problem of consent that Barnett identified by arguing that each generation gives its ongoing consent by debating *constitutional construction*. It is our vibrant constitutional culture, in which the people themselves debate in the public arena what the Constitution means or ought to mean today, that lends it a kind of contemporary democratic legitimacy.

Balkin writes, for example, that over time, "Americans try to persuade each other about the best meaning of constitutional text and principle in current circumstances. These debates and political struggles also help generate Americans' investment in the Constitution as their Constitution, even if they never officially consented to it."[14] Elsewhere he writes, "In every generation, We the People of the United States make the Constitution our own by calling upon its text and its principles and arguing about what they mean in our own time."[15]

Thus, consent to the Constitution is an ongoing process that takes the shape of changing constitutional understandings. These constitutional constructions themselves are legitimate, Balkin claims, because of their responsiveness to democratic politics over time: "[T]he initial authority of the text comes from the fact that it was created through successive acts of popular sovereignty.... The authority of constitutional constructions, in turn, comes from their direct or long-run responsiveness to popular will as expressed through the processes of democratic politics."[16]

In short: the Constitution is premised on *democracy*, and thus any constitutional theory must aim at *democratic* legitimacy. Balkin argues that his theory provides just such legitimacy because it is the very act of debating constitutional construction that makes the Constitution today "our law."[17]

Balkin greatly echoes John Hart Ely (pronounced Ee-lee), whom we shall briefly encounter again in the final chapter on nonoriginalism. Ely also aimed to make the Constitution more democratically legitimate by making the case that judges should use judicial review as a "representation-reinforcing" function. Judges should issue decisions that "[clear] the channels of political change on the one hand, and ... [correct]

certain kinds of discrimination against minorities on the other," for that would be "entirely supportive" of "the underlying premises of the American system of representative democracy."[18] Ely thought judges could make American democracy better if they focused on process.

Although Ely never professed to be an originalist, he thought originalism – or at least the Constitution's text and structure – would justify his approach to judicial review. He claimed that the original Constitution was overwhelmingly concerned with process and democratic governance. He wrote, for example, that "[t]he original Constitution's more pervasive strategy ... can be loosely styled a strategy of pluralism"; that "the concept of representation ... had been at the core of our Constitution from the beginning"; that the colonists were mainly concerned with representative fairness; and that "the original Constitution was principally, indeed I would say overwhelmingly, dedicated to concerns of process and structure and not to the identification and preservation of specific substantive values."[19] Ely admitted that "on [his] more expansive days" he is tempted to claim that his view "represents the ultimate interpretivism" – i.e., his views are consistent with the text and structure of the original Constitution.[20]

To be sure, Ely's theory is not the same as Balkin's. Ely claimed that originalism would basically justify a process-oriented approach to judicial review because the Founders were most concerned with creating a functioning representative democracy. Balkin's slightly different claim is that the Constitution is legitimate because it in fact requires the people themselves to update their understandings of the Constitution in successive eras.

Balkin's view of legitimacy and Ely's instinct to focus on democratic process make a lot of sense. One may disagree with Balkin on the specifics, but surely our Constitution must be democratic at least in *some* respects. It must be responsive to contemporary majorities to some degree. Would we have it any other way? The question for us today as Americans, and for originalists seeking to understand the Constitution's legitimacy, is whether the Constitution *is in fact* sufficiently responsive to contemporary majorities.

Many liberals, after all, think that the Constitution is outdated and is not responsive. Consider Sandy Levinson's book, *Our Undemocratic Constitution*. He thinks that the Constitution is not democratically legitimate when one considers the unamendable and disproportionate Senate, the Electoral College, the presidential veto power, the lifetime tenure of Supreme Court Justices, and the ability of a mere thirteen states to block a constitutional amendment.[21]

Balkin believes that the Constitution, as originally understood, *is* sufficiently responsive to contemporary democratic majorities because the Framers wrote such broad provisions into it so that We the People can continue to debate how the Constitution should be interpreted today. How else could we interpret grand principles such as "Equal Protection of the Laws" and "Due Process of Law" or the broad standards such as "unreasonable searches and seizures"?

Now, surely the Constitution does create *some* form of democracy. We do not have a pure democracy, but we do have some form of republican government. We elect our representatives; the winner of the Electoral College is at a minimum the choice of a nationally distributed majority (even if she doesn't always win the popular vote); we have a large measure of local government at the level of states and municipalities; and our representatives decide on questions usually with a majority vote. But there are undeniably at least some layers separating the people from directly controlling the activities of government.

The key point for a critic such as Levinson is that these layers of separation are enshrined in a constitution that is incredibly difficult to change. Here is where Balkin disagrees, and why Balkin considers himself an originalist: the Founders expected us to update the Constitution through more ways than one. The amendment process is one way, certainly, but the standards and principles in the Constitution afford us a more ready way to "update" its applications.

Of course Balkin is right at a high level of generality – the Constitution has to be updated to new circumstances. The Framers expected that. A conservative or libertarian would fully acknowledge that just because the Framers could never conceive of the Internet does not mean the First Amendment does not apply to it. Just because they did not know about cell phones does not mean the Fourth Amendment cannot be applied to new technologies. And so on. The question for most originalists is whether Balkin reads *too much* into the Constitution's grand provisions. Yes, due process of law is a great principle, but it also had technical legal meaning. The Constitution's standards and principles always admit of new *applications*, but a more conservative originalist might say that Balkin treats them too flexibly to lead to more progressive results. It is not our present task to decide whether Balkin takes his point too far. For our purposes, it is enough to recognize that the notion of a Constitution that allows for updating is certainly sound. Indeed, such a notion was essential if the Constitution was ever to succeed.

THE CONSERVATIVE THEORY: POPULAR SOVEREIGNTY

The most prominent theory of the Constitution's legitimacy is popular sovereignty. Most originalists today — as with most conservative political thinkers generally – believe that some form of popular sovereignty justifies constitutional obedience. The idea is familiar, if not intuitive, to most Americans: "We the People" enacted the Constitution in a public act of ratification, and because the Constitution is thus clothed with the consent of the governed, we must continue to adhere to it today. We may, of course, always call for another constitutional convention or pursue the amendment process to enact constitutional change. Until the Constitution is changed in one of those two ways (and the Constitution *has* been changed several times through the amendment process), we owe it our obedience because "We the People" consented to it.

Michael McConnell, a prominent originalist academic and former federal judge, has explained popular sovereignty thus: "The people's representatives have a right to govern, so long as they do not transgress limits on their authority that are fairly traceable to the constitutional precommitments *of the people themselves*, as reflected directly through text and history, or indirectly through longstanding practice and precedent."[22] Justice Antonin Scalia, perhaps the Supreme Court Justice that has worked the hardest to advance the cause of originalism, evinced a similar commitment to popular sovereignty: it is because the people themselves have imposed certain constraints on the future that makes those constraints binding.[23]

Recall that these are views of popular sovereignty that the previous two schools of thought have rejected. Randy Barnett wrote that popular sovereignty can't possibly clothe a constitution with legitimacy if that constitution does not protect natural rights unless the people unanimously consent to it. And unanimous consent is impossible. Non-originalists point further to the familiar criticism that even if our ancestors could bind us today, the authors and ratifiers of the Constitution were just a bunch of white men and excluded many others from the constitution-making process. But let us put all that aside for the moment. We will get to these criticisms a bit later. First, let us try to understand more fully this idea of popular sovereignty.

Keith Whittington gives a rather comprehensive account of this ground for constitutional legitimacy in his book on originalism.[24] Like Barnett and Epstein, he rejects the notion of tacit consent. *That* cannot be the basis for popular sovereignty. The whole point of popular sovereignty necessarily rejects the idea of tacit consent. Popular sovereignty requires that we make a *choice* about who governs. Quietly acquiescing to an existing situation is not making a choice. If it were otherwise, then tacit consent would just as well justify an absolute monarch so long as the people did not speak out or rebel. But that is not what we mean by popular sovereignty.

So how do we the people *today* give our consent to the Constitution? Are we somehow a part of the popular sovereignty of the founding generation? Or can their act of popular sovereignty bind us today? Two questions must be addressed for a satisfactory theory of popular sovereignty: (1) How is a future people a part of a past people? (2) What must the past act of popular sovereignty have looked like? Is it sufficient that state conventions adopted the Constitution, and not the people through direct vote? Is popular sovereignty a legitimate act if several constituent parts of the society are excluded from it (such as women and slaves)? We must be satisfied both that the initial act of popular sovereignty was legitimate and that we are somehow a part of that act today.

We are a part of the initial act of popular sovereignty, Whittington argues, because "We the People" always have the *potential* to engage in a new act of popular sovereignty by amending the Constitution (or rewriting it entirely). We the people thus give real consent each time we amend the Constitution, just as the founding generation gave its real consent when it ratified the Constitution. Whittington writes that we can abandon the notion of tacit consent in favor of this notion of "potential" sovereignty.

Another way to put this argument is through the metaphor of inertia. We the People in 1789 set the Constitution in motion with our act of consent. It stays in motion until acted upon by another force – a new act of consent. This consent occurs through the amendment process. Whittington summarizes:

> Consensual government does not require the imagination of a current consent; rather, it requires that government receive authorization for its actions. The Constitution provides that authorization. Government action requiring different authorization would require another such expression of consent. The government was set in motion by consent, but it need not demonstrate our continuing consent in order to remain in motion. It is enough that it not change course or even stop its motion, except by our new consent. The implication is that the founders initiated the Constitution, which remains valid and binding not by virtue of their right to govern over us but by virtue of the "historical accident" that their text is the most recent expression of consent.[25]

Thus, Whittington adopts the view of "democratic dualism," which maintains that the "people emerge at particular historical moments to deliberate on constitutional issues and to provide binding expressions of their will, which are to serve as fundamental law in the future when the sovereign is absent."[26]

This inertia theory of popular sovereignty makes a lot of sense. We can see that there is really no other way about it through a process of elimination. We might hypothesize that a world of perfect popular sovereignty would be the world in which all the people deliberate over every decision of society. But that is impossible. A slightly less perfect scheme of popular sovereignty would then be popular authorization for a constitution that creates a system of government that does not require universal participation for all public policy deliberations.

And so that is the system we have. But if we can't consent to every decision for ourselves, is popular sovereignty really a basis for legitimacy? The libertarians would argue that we must abandon popular sovereignty altogether. But that, I fear, is to let the perfect be the enemy of the good. It surely does not follow that, just because the best cannot be attained, the best *practicable* achievement is somehow unworthy or insufficient. If we buy the idea, Lockean in its origin, that the natural equality of all people in the state of nature requires some sort of popular authorization for a system of government, then it makes sense to settle for the best of the attainable expressions of popular sovereignty. And the best practicable expression of popular sovereignty is one in which the people always have the potential to engage in acts of popular sovereignty, and until they do so, their most recent expressions of popular sovereignty continue to govern.

That's all well and good, but what if the *initial* act of popular sovereignty was flawed? The constitution-making and ratification process excluded blacks, women, Native Americans, the property-less, and so on. In his popular defense of the Founding, *Vindicating the Founders*, Thomas G. West quotes numerous historians and political scientists on this point. One wrote, for example, that the "sublime principles of the Declaration did not apply to [blacks]," but were "for whites only."[27] And Paul Brest, in his famous law review article attacking originalism, wrote, "The drafting, adopting, or amending of the Constitution may itself have suffered from defects of democratic process which detract from its moral claims. To take an obvious example, the interests of black Americans were not adequately represented in the adoption of the Constitution of 1787 or the fourteenth amendment."[28]

There is no doubt that by today's standards, the initial act of founding would be considered in this sense illegitimate. But by this reasoning, nothing that *ever* occurred in the past would be legitimate so long as some injustices of this sort existed. Was the freeing of the slaves in the Civil War Amendments illegitimate because women could not yet vote? Every time that we come to understand that a certain voice in society ought to be heard, does that make all prior acts on the part of society illegitimate? That would be absurd.

Indeed, even if we re-ratified the Constitution *today* with a more inclusive process, who is to say that *that* process will be legitimate in the ultimate sense of that word? Perhaps in one hundred years we will come to realize that another group should have participated in the ratification process. Perhaps we will come to realize that there was some latent defect in twenty-first-century America that we simply cannot yet conceive of today. How would we ever know that the process of moral evolution has been complete? How does one know that one has reached the end of history?

We must instead judge historical acts within the context of their times. And although many progressives continue to charge that the Founders were somehow backward and ignorant people, they were remarkably progressive for their time. And that is all that matters. Yes, they had to make an accommodation with slavery. But before the Founding no one had ever written down in a founding document that all men are created equal. The Founders must be given tremendous credit for even accomplishing that extraordinary act. And all leading founders did, as Tom West explains, find slavery abhorrent and continued to say so. But they owned that, *at the time*, they had no *immediate* solution for the extermination of *all* slavery.

Consider that few colonists discussed the evils of slavery at all prior to the Revolution. But after Thomas Jefferson penned his famous words – that all men are created equal – Americans started to question how slavery comported with their notions of equality. Unsurprisingly, as West describes, *over half the states* abolished slavery after 1776. That in and of itself, while imperfect, was tremendous progress. The Constitution would end the slave trade by 1808 – a full decade *after* all but one state had already abolished the slave trade. Many states beefed up laws for the protection of the life of blacks, for example by treating the murder of a black slave the same as the murder of a free white.

It may even be that the Founders, by accommodating the Southern states, helped bring about the end of slavery. From their point of view, slavery would continue to exist one way or another. Either it would exist in the South in states that were at least part of the Union, over which the Northern states had some control; or slavery would exist in those same regions in an independent confederacy over which the Northern states had no control. The Founders chose the lesser of two evils, and thus did the best they could for the conditions under which they lived. Those who claim the Founding was illegitimate because they could not achieve perfection are imposing an arrogant, ahistorical standard. They exhibit what the socialist historian E. P. Thompson once called "the enormous condescension of posterity."

These three arguments – that the Founders actually made tremendous progress for the times in which they lived; that if their act was illegitimate, then all prior acts would have to be considered illegitimate; and that we can never know if any modern acts are legitimate because we cannot know whether we have reached the end of history – demonstrate that we must keep things in perspective. The Founding was as legitimate as could be for its time. Indeed, it was pathbreaking. And perhaps just as critically, the Constitution the Founders created has allowed us better to redeem its founding promises by amendments that have sought over time to remedy many of its original defects.

Accepting popular sovereignty, to recap, requires a two-step argument: first, we must be convinced that the initial act was just, and second, we must be convinced that this initial act matters at all. West's book and the argument just described go to the first step. Whittington's solution goes to the second: the Founders' expression of legitimate consent is the most recent expression of the consent of We the People, which is binding on us until we amend it.

NEXT STEPS

Some might not be convinced by any of the theories of constitutional legitimacy just presented – the natural rights theory, the democratic theory, or the popular sovereignty theory. Perhaps one might think that each of these views is too narrow or too flawed. Would we be justified in obeying a constitution that fully protected natural rights but which created a constitutional monarchy? And what if we think the Constitution does not adequately protect natural rights anyway? The same questions can be applied to the democratic grounds for legitimacy: Would a democratic constitution that completely trammeled our natural rights compel our obedience? And what if our Constitution does not create a very democratic system (thinking about the Senate, Electoral College, and so on)? Lastly, we might not be convinced that a popular sovereignty theory of constitutional legitimacy can overcome the flaws in the initial act of ratification.

Before we decide that each of these theories must be thrown out, let us see what the Founders themselves had to say about our Constitution's legitimacy. Their views surely cannot bootstrap themselves into acceptance. But maybe their views are more persuasive to us. After all, the Founders had to declare the causes that impelled them to the separation from Great Britain. They had to think long and hard about what justified such a break. Let us see what they had to say.

4   THE FOUNDERS ON FOUNDING

"The *improvements* made by the dead form a debt against the living, who take the benefit of them."[1]

James Madison, Letter to Thomas Jefferson (1790)

The Founders, I claim here, understood constitutional legitimacy to include each of our three grounds for legitimacy: natural rights, democratic government, and popular sovereignty. But their understanding also transcends them all. The Founders understood that the Constitution they framed may have been flawed with respect to each ground for legitimacy. Nevertheless, they argued, prudence justifies adherence to the whole. That, at least, is what James Madison suggests in his understudied response to Jefferson's "dead hand of the past" letter. If we are unpersuaded by the natural rights theory, the progressive democratic theory, or the popular sovereignty theory of the Constitution's legitimacy standing alone, then this more holistic view of the Founders may persuade us.

THE DECLARATION OF INDEPENDENCE

What better place to start our search than in the very document through which our Founders declared they had a right to break from their old loyalties? Reading the Declaration of Independence, written in 1776 at the dawn of the American Revolution, to understand the principles of the Constitution, written in 1787, is not an uncontroversial proposition. For many years it was fashionable among political scientists and students of American history to argue that the

Constitution of 1787 was a conservative, reactionary repudiation of the democratic principles of 1776.[2]

I am not convinced. There is no doubt that the so-called Critical Period from 1776 to 1787, in which the states experimented with exceedingly democratic forms of government and the Articles of Confederation established at best a loose union among the states, informed the making of the Constitution. We shall see momentarily how the Framers reacted to the tribulations of this period. The Constitutional Convention convened because states were not guaranteeing the obligations of contract with respect to debtors. The Congress could not requisition the necessary military supplies and personnel from the states. Neither could it successfully raise money under Articles of Confederation. The delegates to the Convention sought to create a frame of government that would increase national powers to remedy these real inadequacies. Insofar as the Constitution reined in democratic excesses by creating checks and balances and a separation of powers, and insofar as it guaranteed the rights of creditors by guaranteeing the obligations of contracts generally, the Constitution was surely a reaction to the problems of the time.

But it hardly follows that in writing a specific structure of government the Framers rejected the *principles* that underlay the Declaration of Independence. Separation of powers is not incompatible with democracy. The Framers believed that separation of powers, checks and balances, and other limits were necessary for the very survival of democracy. We would therefore be remiss to ignore the Declaration in our quest to understand how the Founders understood the legitimacy of the Constitution they created. Madison himself invoked the Declaration of Independence in *The Federalist Papers* when justifying the authority of the Convention to propose a new constitution that would "abolish or alter their governments as to them shall seem most likely to effect their safety and happiness."[3] And Bernard Bailyn has defended the Framers and their work as being consistent with the ideological origins of the American Revolution.[4]

Indeed, in the Declaration the Founders felt that they must "declare the causes which impel them to the separation" from the political bands that had previously connected them, and thus it manifestly provides insight into general notions of political legitimacy at the time of the Founding. Only foundational principles could justify such a drastic action. By the end of this chapter I hope we will come to see that the Constitution and the purposes for which it was written evoke the same principles at play in the Declaration.

What, in the minds of the author and signers of the Declaration, made such a break from their previous bonds legitimate? The key clause is well known but also too often overlooked: all men are created equal; they are endowed with unalienable rights including the right to life, liberty, and the pursuit of happiness; and "[t]hat to secure these rights, Governments are instituted among Men, deriving their just powers from the consent of the governed." In this one line the Founders offered the two most crucial bases for constitutional legitimacy: government must derive its power from the consent of the governed – a social contract of sorts – and it must secure our unalienable rights. In one fell swoop – at least if we buy the Founders' account – we see that perhaps both the libertarian originalists and the popular sovereignty conservatives simplify their grounds for constitutional legitimacy. The Constitution must be rooted in an act of popular sovereignty *and* it must protect our natural rights.

The Declaration does not stop there, however. The government, it implies, must not only derive its powers from the consent of the governed, but must also continue to rule by self-government. That is, it must constitute a democratic or republican form of government. In the long chain of usurpations and abuses listed in the Declaration – the acts that justified separation from Great Britain – Jefferson, the Declaration's primary author, wrote that King George III had refused to pass laws "for the accommodation of large districts of people, unless those people would relinquish the right of Representation in the Legislature, a right inestimable to them and formidable to tyrants only."[5] Furthermore, Jefferson wrote, the King "has called together legislative bodies at places unusual, uncomfortable, and distant from the depository of their public Records"[6] and he has "dissolved Representative Houses repeatedly."[7] He has refused to cause other legislatures to be elected, and thus the legislative powers "have returned to the People at large for their exercise."[8] And more specifically, he has kept standing armies without the people's consent and has taxed them without their consent.[9]

This train of abuses suggests that for a government to be legitimate at all, the people must be permitted to govern themselves in their own legislatures. Legitimate government, then, requires representative government. The Declaration of Independence thus gives us an indication of everything the Constitution, in the mind of the Founders, must accomplish to be legitimate: it must derive its powers from the consent of the governed; it must secure the just ends of government; and it must create a representative or democratic form of government.

We will soon explore each of these bases for legitimacy with an in-depth look at what the Founders said at the Constitutional Convention, what they wrote in defense of the Constitution as it was being publicly debated during ratification, and their other writings generally. Before doing so, I cannot resist addressing one particular criticism of taking the Declaration of Independence seriously as a statement of principles. Progressives who dislike the natural rights principles in the Declaration often argue that it was merely a "legal brief" and therefore its authors threw in, almost willy-nilly, every possible argument they could conceive that would justify separating from Great Britain. No more dignified than throwing darts at a board.

John Hart Ely made such an argument. He wrote that the Declaration of Independence was like a legal brief and that "[p]eople writing briefs are likely, and often well advised, to throw in arguments of every hue." Specifically, "People writing briefs for revolution are obviously unlikely to have apparent positive law on their side, and are therefore well advised to rely on natural law."[10] Therefore, Ely argued, we ought not take their invocation of natural law very seriously.

That reasoning does not seem persuasive. In the first place, it is very likely that in justifying a break from positive law obligations, the Founders, as I've suggested, had to think long and hard about what gave them the right to do so. They believed they *had* to appeal to natural rights because that was what was necessary for their act to be legitimate. That, it seems to me, reinforces rather than undermines the conclusion that a constitution must protect natural rights to be legitimate. But more importantly, we should always be suspicious of those who would read natural rights out of the Declaration but rely on it to justify the necessity of democratic legitimacy. Ely's criticism, after all, could be lodged against his own justification for constitutional legitimacy. That is, if we should not take Declaration's natural rights claims seriously, why take its consent-of-the-governed claims seriously? Indeed, Ely cited the

Declaration for his proposition that the Founders were overwhelmingly concerned with consent and representative government, but then ignored the natural rights language.

NATURAL RIGHTS AND SELF-GOVERNMENT

When the Founders debated the Constitution at the Convention, and when the people debated it in the throes of ratification, these same themes repeated. It could not be doubted that the Constitution had to be republican; it had to "enable" self-government to be legitimate. As James Madison wrote in *Federalist* No. 39,

> The first question that offers itself is, whether the general form and aspect of the government be strictly republican. It is evident that no other form would be reconcilable with the genius of the people of America; with the fundamental principles of the Revolution; or with that honorable determination which animates every votary of freedom, to rest all our political experiments on the capacity of mankind for self-government. If the plan of the convention, therefore, be found to depart from the republican character, its advocates must abandon it as no longer defensible.[11]

John Adams, in his *Thoughts on Government*, likewise declared that "principles and reasonings ... will convince any candid mind that there is no good government but what is republican."[12] As one great historian of the Founding, Gordon Wood, has written, "For most Americans ... this was the deeply felt meaning of the Revolution: they had created a new world, a republican world. No one doubted that the new polities would be republics." That meant instituting an elective system of government.[13]

Yet the Framers did not want total self-government. From the first instance at the Convention they rejected man's capacity for pure democracy. Two days after the Virginia Plan was proposed in the Convention, Mr. Gerry, one of the most Whiggish delegates, said, "The evils we experience flow from the excess of democracy. The people do not want virtue; but are the dupes of pretended patriots."[14] Mr. Mason agreed, "admitt[ing] that we had been too democratic," though he "was afraid we [should] incautiously run into the opposite extreme."[15] These are telling statements from two delegates who would come to oppose the Constitution on the ground that it did not adequately safeguard the rights of the people; even the more "democratic" delegates believed the Union could not long survive on the principle of pure democracy. Mr. Randolph, another who refused to sign the Constitution, observed that same day that the general object of the Senate "was to provide a cure for the evils under which the U.S. laboured; that in tracing these evils to their origin every man had found it in the turbulence and follies of democracy: that some check therefore was to be sought for [against] this tendency of our Government."[16]

Of course the Constitution had to create a democracy; it had to be republican in form. But democracy had to be saved from itself. A pure democracy would not long survive. The rights of the people could easily be abused in a democratic system. The Founders sought a solution for this problem: they sought to create a system that would both be democratic and protect natural rights.

The solution adopted by the Constitution is now famous. The large sphere over which the federal republic could extend would mitigate the factional spirit of smaller republics by making it more difficult for a faction to possess the opinion of a majority of the people. As Madison writes in *Federalist* No. 10, representation, an improvement over pure democracy, allows for two advantages. First, it will carve out a sphere for virtue because the body of men to which the people delegate authority will "refine and enlarge" the public views.[17] The people usually do not have the wisdom, and surely they do not have the time, to devote themselves to the careful study of public affairs. They are thus likely to be led astray. But the people's representatives, chosen specifically for that purpose, could devote themselves to such study.

Second, a republic can extend over a larger territory – it is very hard to do things by direct democracy in a society of, say, 300 million people. But a republican government can extend over a larger territory and people. The advantage of the larger territory is that a single factional impulse will be less likely to actuate the spirit of a majority.[18] An old adage captures the reasoning: you can fool some people some of the time, but you can't fool all people all of the time. The larger the polity, the harder it is to fool a majority.

But these two principles of delegating governing responsibility to a select body of men and of extending the size of the country must go together. A large territory by itself does not protect the rights of the people. But neither does representation: Madison believed the state legislatures then existing were actuated by a spirit of faction.[19] The solution, then, must be to combine the principle of representation with the benefits of the larger extent of territory over which that same principle allows a republican government to rule. In this way the republican principle can remedy the effect of faction because the diversity of faction would make it rare that any one attained a permanent majority.

Thus republicanism over an extended territory would save self-government. But there is a third piece still missing. The people's rights still had to be protected even from the temporary passions expressed in *republican* majorities. Our representatives can still trample our rights – as they so often do today. Representation and large territory are two crucial mechanisms for the protection of rights, but there are even more protections that the Framers could and did implement. They intended to restrain republican institutions themselves with checks and balances,[20] federalism,[21] and separation of powers.[22] These protections were meant to check republican decision-making as much as republicanism itself would be a check on democracy; they were meant to create a certain form of republicanism that remedied the vices of popular government.

From this cursory account it appears that the libertarian-originalist view of constitutional legitimacy is not how the Founders understood it; the Constitution could not merely protect natural rights. More was required. Likewise, the Founders believed the Constitution had to be fundamentally republican to be legitimate, but not purely republican, in the same way that it could not be purely democratic. Thus the progressive theorists who focus on "reinforcing" representation or "enabling" self-government through current debates over constitutional construction are surely partly right: the Constitution must create a system responsive to contemporary democratic majorities. But that was only one aspect of the Constitution's legitimacy in the mind of the Founders.

POPULAR SOVEREIGNTY

The Founders believed that the Constitution needed both to establish a republican form of government and to protect natural rights; but they also believed that to be legitimate, the Constitution *itself* needed to be rooted firmly in the consent of the governed. This is our third ground for constitutional legitimacy: popular sovereignty. This notion of popular sovereignty has very different implications than the notions of self-government, representation, or rule by the general will of the people. Because even legislators cannot be trusted not to abuse their power, and thus properly to discharge the people's will, the consent of the governed is necessary at a moment of founding to restrain the powers of the legislators to ensure they act more consonantly with the true interests and will of the people themselves.

The Declaration of Independence was the most definitive declaration of the right of popular, rather than some other kind of, sovereignty. The government derives its just powers from the *consent of the governed.* Leading men from the Founding period repeatedly insisted on this point. James Otis declared in 1764 that "supreme absolute power is *originally* and *ultimately* in the people; and they never did in fact *freely*, nor can they *rightfully* make an absolute, unlimited renunciation of this divine right."[23] Samuel Adams declared in 1772 that "[w]hen Men enter into Society, it is by voluntary consent; and they have a right to demand and insist upon the performance of such conditions, And previous limitations as form an equitable *original compact.*"[24] Thomas Paine adumbrated the origins of civil society in his pamphlet *Common Sense.* When the defect in the moral virtue of individuals reveals the necessity of establishing a government, men will create a convention or assembly to deliberate over the form of government. "In this first parliament," he writes, "every man by natural right will have a seat."[25]

To take two last examples, Alexander Hamilton wrote in 1775 that "the origin of all civil government, justly established, must be a voluntary compact, between the rulers and the ruled; and must be liable to such limitations, as are necessary for the security of the *absolute rights* of the latter"; for, he asks, "what original title can any man or set of men

have, to govern others, except their own consent?"[26] Thomas Tudor
Tucker, an early pamphleteer to develop the idea of a constitution
rooted in consent of the governed as the proper mechanism for
restraining rulers, wrote in 1784: "All authority is derived from the
people at large, held only during their pleasure, and exercised only for
their benefit," and therefore "the privileges of the legislative branches
ought to be defined by the constitution," which must itself be "the
avowed act of the people at large."[27] "It should be the first and
fundamental law of the State, and should prescribe the limits of all
delegated power. It should be declared to be paramount to all acts of
the Legislature, and irrepealable and unalterable by any authority but
the express consent of a majority of the citizens collected by such
regular mode as may be therein provided."[28]

In the *The Federalist Papers*, Madison presumed the legitimacy of
this sovereignty and its necessity for forming a new government. In
Federalist No. 38, he argued that America "has been sensible of her
malady" and "has obtained a regular and unanimous advice from men
of her own deliberate choice."[29] Hamilton also relied on the ultimate
legitimacy of popular sovereignty when he declared that "it seems
to have been reserved to the people of this country ... to decide the
important question, whether societies of men are really capable or
not of establishing good government from reflection and choice, or
whether they are forever destined to depend for their political constitution on accident and force."[30] Madison reminded us, finally, that
"the people are the only legitimate fountain of power, and it is from
them that the constitutional character ... is derived."[31]

Ratification is consonant with this view of popular sovereignty.
Madison wrote that ratification appears to be both a federal and a
national act: "the Constitution is to be founded on the assent and
ratification of the people of America, given by deputies elected for
the special purpose," but it is also derived from "the assent and
ratification of the several States," whose powers are themselves derived
from "the authority of the people themselves." The Constitution still
depended on the authority not of the state governments acting through
state legislatures, but "by that of the people themselves."[32] In his final
extended discussion on the ratification provision, Madison argued that
it "speaks for itself": "The express authority of the people alone could

give due validity to the Constitution."[33] Hamilton suggested, moreover, that ratification by the people is a distinct advantage of the Constitution over the Articles of Confederation, which was ratified by the states.[34]

Madison later added that without the ratification process the Constitution would be nothing; whether just or republican does not alone make the Constitution binding. It still needs the assent of the people. The proposed Constitution is "of no more consequence than the paper on which it is written, unless it be stamped with the approbation of those to whom it is addressed."[35] The Convention bore in mind that the "plan to be framed and proposed was to be submitted to *the people themselves*, the disapprobation of this supreme authority would destroy it forever; its approbation blot out antecedent errors and irregularities."[36] James Wilson agreed. When responding to charges that the Convention exceeded its authority, he argued, "I think the late Convention has done nothing beyond their powers." The Constitution "is laid before the citizens . . . to be judged by the natural, civil and political rights of men. By their *fiat*, it will become of value and authority; without it, it will never receive the character of authenticity and power."[37]

Popular sovereignty, or at least popular ratification of fundamental constitutions, was still a relatively new concept when the Constitution was drafted. Between 1776 and 1778 twelve state constitutions were enacted, ten by ordinary legislation and two by special convention. None was submitted to popular ratification.[38] Indeed, the Framers at first attempted to offer justifications for their authority on the basis of the sovereignty of the several states, even though Madison insisted on popular sovereignty early on.[39] It was not until later in their deliberations that "their focus shifted to the legitimating effect of popular ratification and a theory of popular sovereignty." [40]

Gordon Wood, in his seminal work on the creation of the American republic, illustrates with myriad examples from the Founding period this new understanding of popular sovereignty requiring an initial social compact restraining even the people's legislators.[41] Wood explains why this concept was so new and took time to develop: "[S]ince the legislatures, as the legitimate representatives, were the spokesmen for the people in the society, it was difficult, if not impossible, without a new conception of representation to deny them the right to alter or to construe the constitutions as they saw fit when the needs of the society demanded."[42] Yet just such a new conception of representation was necessary because of the widespread disquietude over the unjust acts of the state legislatures in the Critical Period. Americans grew more and more dissatisfied with "the fairest and fullest representative legislatures in the world."[43]

The important point to understand is that popular sovereignty, as the Founding generation understood it, was not equivalent to direct rule by the people or even representative rule by the people. It was the people's very representatives who were violating the rights of the people. Thus, rule by the general will of the legislature was an inadequate expression of the true will of the whole people. Because the people could not rule themselves properly even through the most representative of governments, to be truly sovereign they had to delimit the power of the government in a contract.

We can now summarize. The Founders had a commitment to self-government as well as to natural rights, and thus likely intended to write a constitution that would enable democratic majorities to rule but also protect their natural rights. Thus, the Constitution, to be legitimate, would need to make some kind of compromise between the protection of natural rights and republican rule for legitimacy. But the Founders also believed that, through the initial act of popular sovereignty, the people in the past would explicitly bind the future – including republican majorities – to their will. The Constitution, then, had to be republican, had to protect natural rights, and had to be rooted in an initial act of popular sovereignty.

PRUDENCE AND THE PROBLEM OF FOUNDING

But might the Constitution be flawed with respect to any of these grounds for legitimacy? We have seen how some argue the initial ratification was defective because segments of the population, such as women and slaves, were excluded from the process. The Constitution also may not have been – and it may not be – sufficiently republican or sufficiently protective of natural rights to satisfy others. Put simply, especially if the Constitution or its ratification were flawed, why does one generation, long dead and gone, have a right to bind another? This difficult problem is what we have already described as Jefferson's "dead hand of the past."[44]

The answer to Jefferson may be more intuitive than one might think: founding a government is extremely difficult and the exercise should rarely be repeated. That is how James Madison understood the challenge of founding and it was his answer to Jefferson. Because many scholars continue to invoke Jefferson for the dead-hand proposition, it is only fitting that we explore the views of the Founder who directly responded to him.

Jefferson's formulation of the problem of a perpetual constitution is well known, and we quoted it in the Introduction: "The question Whether one generation of men has a right to bind another, seems never to have been started either on this or our side of the water," he wrote Madison from Paris. "Yet it is a question of such consequences as not only to merit decision, but place also, among the fundamental principles of every government....I set out on this ground, which I suppose to be self evident, '*that the earth belongs in usufruct to the living*;' that the dead have neither powers nor rights over it."[45]

Madison's response is less known. In it he argues that certain past acts can bind the living. He writes:

> If the earth be the gift of *nature* to the living, their title can extend to the earth in its *natural* state only. The *improvements* made by the dead form a debt against the living, who take the benefit of them. This debt cannot be otherwise discharged than by a proportionate obedience to the will of the Authors of the improvements.[46]

Madison specifically mentions repelling conquest, "the evils of which descend through many generations," as an example of forming a debt against the living. Indeed, why should men sacrifice their lives – or their fortunes or sacred honor for that matter – if posterity did not maintain the just fruits of their sacrifices? If posterity had no obligations to the past, why should past generations fight so hard for the liberty of their progeny?

The Constitution was formed on the heels of a bloody revolution – for that reason alone it might form a debt against the living generation. But what is more, Madison's claim extends to constitution-making itself.

As with repelling conquest, the act of creating a Constitution forms a debt against future generations. The act is so fundamental in the history of any society, so difficult and yet so critical, that the living generation cannot but be bound to its imperatives in at least some ways.

Madison elaborates on these features of constitution-making in *Federalist* No. 37 and No. 38. In the former, he writes of the necessity of "sacrific[ing] theoretical propriety to the force of extraneous considerations."[47] He states:

> The history of almost all the great councils and consultations held among mankind for reconciling their discordant opinions, assuaging their mutual jealousies, and adjusting their respective interests, is a history of factions, contentions, and disappointments, and may be classed among the most dark and degrading pictures which display the infirmities and depravities of the human character.[48]

In short, Madison argues that founding is an extremely challenging enterprise. It should not be too often repeated. In surveying the turbulent history of foundings in *Federalist* No. 38, he concludes,

> If these lessons teach us, on one hand, to admire the improvement made by America on the ancient mode of preparing and establishing regular plans of government, they serve not less, on the other, to admonish us of the hazards and difficulties incident to such experiments, and of the great imprudence of unnecessarily multiplying them.[49]

It is prudence that, for Madison, justifies ignoring the imperfections of the Constitution. Prudence itself lends support to the proposition that the Constitution is a legitimate document – even if it is imperfectly legitimate with respect to other bases of legitimacy.

Madison's concern for prudence can perhaps be reformulated in terms of another notion that is required for constitutional or political legitimacy: stability. "Stability in government," writes Madison in *Federalist* No. 37, "is essential to national character and to the advantages annexed to it, as well as to that repose and confidence in the minds of the people, which are among the chief blessings of civil society."[50] Although here he is discussing the balance of energy and stability provided by the constitutional structure of the new government, his reasoning applies to constitutionalism itself. How legitimate would the Constitution be were it subject to the vicissitudes of temporary passions and opinions, if it were constantly mutable?

This concern for stability motivated Madison to warn in *Federalist* No. 49 against unnecessarily multiplying the "reference of constitutional questions to the decision of the whole society."[51] We do not want the people continuously to change the Constitution because, "as every appeal to the people would carry an implication of some defect in the government, frequent appeals would, in a great measure, deprive the government of that veneration which time bestows on every thing, and without which perhaps the wisest and freest governments would not possess the *requisite stability*."[52] Stability, understood as a prudential requirement in human affairs, is another requirement for constitutional legitimacy.[53]

We might also note that notwithstanding Jefferson's letter to Madison, the Declaration of Independence that Jefferson himself authored is in fact consistent with Madison's view of stability and prudence. The Declaration states that when it becomes *necessary* for a people to dissolve the political bands that had previously connected them, a decent respect to the opinions of mankind requires that they declare the causes that impel them to the separation.[54] The Declaration did not contemplate whimsical dissolution of the existing social order. That order must secure the people's rights to life, liberty, and the pursuit of happiness. It is only when a "Form of Government becomes destructive of these ends" that it is the "Right of the People to alter or to abolish it, and to institute new Government."[55] By the very reasoning and principles of the Declaration, a people, including our generation, does not have an unequivocal right to alter or abolish its government as long as it, on the whole, secures the rights of the people to life, liberty, and the pursuit of happiness.

None of this is to say that Madison or the Framers believed that *any* constitution must be accepted. Indeed, Madison was keenly aware that in the throes of ratification, the federalists were asking the people to reject the government formed by their revolutionary forebears more than a decade earlier on the principles of a long history of revolutionary ideology.[56] To assuage his readers about the novelty of the Constitution, Madison asked in *Federalist* No. 14:

> Is it not the glory of the people of America that, whilst they have
> paid a decent regard to the opinions of former times and other
> nations, they have not suffered a blind veneration for antiquity, for
> custom, or for names, to overrule the suggestions of their own good
> sense, the knowledge of their own situation, and the lessons of their
> own experience? To this manly spirit posterity will be indebted for
> the possession, and the world for the example, of the numerous
> innovations displayed on the American theater in favor of private
> rights and public happiness.[57]

Madison did not believe in blind devotion to antiquity; nor would
he have wanted future generation to have a blind veneration for the
"names" of the Founding generation. In the same way that the Framers
sought to improve on the earlier experiments with state constitutions
and a national government, they expected posterity to continue this
improvement.

But in Madison's passage we find the careful balance between what
he described as a *blind* veneration and a proper indebtedness. Madison
in the same breath said that the "manly spirit" of questioning authority
will create a debt against posterity – a debt owed the Framers due to
their "numerous innovations...in favor of private rights and public
happiness." He believed that for the Constitution to create this indebtedness, it must protect private rights and secure public happiness. It
must, in other words, be good and just. Posterity would surely improve
upon the Framers' accomplishment, just as the Framers improved
upon the accomplishments of the revolutionaries of 1776. But as long
as their frame of government continues to favor our rights and secure
our public happiness, prudence demands an adherence to the political
bands that already unite us.

WHERE WE ARE

We have established a few things. Chapters 3 and 4 offered some
possible grounds for constitutional legitimacy. Some originalists focus
on natural rights; others on its democratic elements; and yet others on
the initial act of popular sovereignty. We saw in this chapter that the
Founders believed that the Constitution had to be legitimate in all three

ways for it to bind the people. Even if the Constitution is imperfect in these respects, however, prudence may also justify adherence to the whole.

It is my view that the Founders are right. If the Constitution protects natural rights, creates a republican form of government, and is rooted in an act of popular sovereignty, then prudence demands that we obey it today, whatever its imperfections. We can always seek to fix such imperfections, after all, through the amendment process. The Founders undertook an almost unfathomably difficult enterprise.

If the Constitution is legitimate, then we also have two possible reasons we should be originalists. The first reason consists in the two-step argument I have previewed from the beginning: (1) we must be originalist because that is the default way to interpret any public human communication, and our legal system gives legal effect to such meanings and (2) the Constitution, as originally understood, is legitimate and worthy of our obedience today.

This is how we assess the continuing validity of *any* law: we first interpret a law on the books, regardless of how far in the past it was enacted, by asking what the law *says* or *means*. This meaning usually will be given full legal effect, although it surely will be subject to other existing rules in the system (such as the rules for attempt, self-defense, or against absurdity). And it is *good* that our system gives legal effect to these words because doing so is necessary for our very conception of the rule of law. Only *after* we've determined the law's meaning and its resultant legal effect do we ask whether this law *still ought to be law*.

I'd like to suggest a second route, however, to the conclusion that we ought to be originalists. Consider that if the original Constitution is just and worthy of our obedience, then it is only *that original Constitution* that we must obey. Not a different Constitution interpreted in some modern, nonoriginalist way. This does not preclude the possibility that some other interpretation may be more legitimate; but someone would have to justify *that* constitution independently, and also justify its deviation from our legal system's approach to the "rule of law."[58] This, indeed, is what I think Madison had in mind when he wrote his letter to Jefferson. He said the Constitution was an "improvement" of the kind that forms a debt against future generations. In other words, he already believed that the Constitution he helped draft was good and legitimate. The only way for posterity to maintain the fruits of that improvement was therefore by a "proportionate obedience to the will of the authors of the improvement" – by originalism.

Whichever of these two approaches we adopt, we have yet to ask: did the Founders succeed? That is, did they manage to create a Constitution whose provisions form a just regime worthy of our continuing obedience today? What, in other words, does the Constitution actually say? What kind of constitutional order does it create?

Though we have not specifically attempted to answer that question, we have gone a long way in answering it in this chapter. We saw that the Founders sought to create a constitution that would be republican and also protect natural rights. They did so by enacting certain structural provision: representation, checks and balances, separation of powers, and federalism. A disquisition on the success of such measures would take a whole other book. Similarly, an analysis of the meaning of the key provisions in the Constitution – the Commerce Clause, the General Welfare Clause, the Privileges or Immunities Clause, and so on – would take yet another. The same goes for any discussion of the key protections in the Bill of Rights, where the Founders specifically protected some of our natural rights (as well as other positive rights).

But surely we can say that the Founders succeeded to a great degree. They created a regime of self-government that has endured for more than two centuries. There may be threats to our liberties and self-government today stemming from nonoriginalist interpretations of the Constitution; for example, many argue that the administrative state combines legislative, judicial, and executive powers and thus undermines the separation of powers. I think that is true. But we are making the case in this book for the *original* Constitution, as its provisions and amendments were originally understood. And although there are times in our history when the three branches combined to infringe on the people's liberties – the Alien & Sedition Acts are a famous example – for much of our history the branches have been checks on one another. We still hear occasional complaints of "gridlock" in Washington, and although effective democracy must be balanced with protection of rights, to a large degree such gridlock reflects the successful operation of the separation of powers.

The larger point is that, to a great extent, our original Constitution, while imperfect, successfully balanced the competing ends of government. It successfully balanced the needs of self-rule with the need to protect natural rights through a variety of structural provisions and substantive protections. The Founders helped create the only nation on the face of the earth that was, in Lincoln's words, conceived in liberty and dedicated to the proposition that all men are created equal. They overcame – for the most part – the passions and prejudices of a turbulent time. I can think of no constitution that has been more successful or more enduring.

5   INTERPRETING THE CONSTITUTION

"[W]e must never forget that it is a *constitution* we are expounding."[1]

Chief Justice John Marshall (1819)

We have seen what the original Constitution does in its broad strokes. It balances the competing ends of government: it creates a democratic regime that also protects natural rights. Now we will see how originalists claim the Constitution should be interpreted in certain cases to advance these core purposes and adhere to its original meaning. It is often said that original meaning only gets us so far – the Constitution will have some indeterminacies because its provisions have some vagueness or ambiguity. Thus, originalism might not always supply us with an answer. Many originalists have argued that in those cases something must supplement original meaning. When that meaning isn't clear, we have to come up with a "construction" – some extra-constitutional way to decide a case.

Here we will see, unsurprisingly, differences among the schools of originalism. Those who are of a more libertarian bent argue that the Constitution should be interpreted with a "presumption of liberty." Randy Barnett made this phrase famous. This interpretive device errs on the side of declaring acts of Congress unconstitutional unless the government meets a burden of showing that the act is both necessary and proper, usually requiring a clear textual basis for the act in the Constitution.

The more politically conservative originalists tend to support a "presumption of constitutionality" interpretation of the Constitution. This presumption derives from the view that the people's representatives in

Congress have a right to legislate unless there is a clear textual prohibition, usually to be found in the restrictions of the Bill of Rights. Such an interpretation would be more generous to Congress (and the state legislatures) than a presumption of liberty would be.

There are some variations on these two positions. Some originalists argue that, to stay true to the competing purposes in the Constitution, we should employ a presumption of liberty when it comes to federal acts, but a presumption of constitutionality when it comes to state acts.[2] After all, the federal government is one of limited and enumerated powers, but the states have plenary police powers. The libertarians think, on the other hand, that the presumption of liberty should apply across the board, and conservatives also often think that the presumption of constitutionality should apply both to state and federal acts.

Finally, some originalists argue there shouldn't be "presumptions" or "constructions" at all. These originalists claim that a rich array of "original interpretive conventions" was used at the time the Constitution was enacted, and that using these original interpretive rules enables us to answer most constitutional questions without resorting to presumptions – or at least without resorting to constitutional "construction."

My view is that the original interpretive conventions approach is certainly the best one, but that it is not so simple. The Founding generation had numerous legal tools to help clarify ambiguities in statutory (or constitutional) meaning, and they expected interpreters to use them. Thus, the number of times when we really won't have an answer to a constitutional question is much smaller than what most advocates of construction seem to think. But that hardly means there will *never* be a question that, after all the tools of interpretation are deployed, we will still be unable to answer. In those instances, even the founding generation debated whether interpreters of the Constitution should use something like a presumption of liberty (what they called a "strict construction" of the Constitution), or something like a presumption of constitutionality. So even "original interpretive conventions" cannot completely avoid the debate between these two presumptions, because there is originalist evidence for both.

Ultimately, the nature of the Constitution – with its enumeration of federal powers and dual sovereignty, with its aim to enable democracy but also to protect natural rights – might require either of these presumptions in different contexts. The bottom line is that the Constitution will have some indeterminacies (even if not that often), and there is still some debate over what we do in those cases. Nevertheless, we should take heart. The Founders had a kind of ultimate interpretive convention: they had a theory of *liquidation*, whereby the Constitution's ambiguities would be resolved over time in particular contexts and previously ambiguous provisions would *become* "fixed" over time. After canvassing the various debates over interpretation and construction, this chapter ends with the Founders' theory of liquidation.

IS CONSTRUCTION NECESSARY?

A brief comment on the terms "interpretation" and "construction" is in order. I have used the terms because they are prominent in the originalist literature and many originalists believe there is a difference between the two. Recall that these originalists argue that the "interpretation" of a written text does not always give an answer to a given question. Sometimes, we just won't know quite whether the text *means* that the act in question is constitutional. The evidence points both ways. But because judges still have to decide the case before them, these originalists will say that judges must at this point choose a "construction" to decide the case.

The "presumption of constitutionality" is one such "construction." The idea is that this construction may not be required by the text of the Constitution. We just choose it because we have to decide the case somehow. A judge who chooses to adopt the presumption of constitutionality will, in cases of doubt, hold an act constitutional. A judge who chooses to adopt the presumption of liberty construction will, in cases of doubt, strike down the act.

It is not obvious to me, however, that there really is a difference between construction and interpretation even as defined by these originalists. Barnett, for example, is one of the most vocal defenders of a distinction between interpretation and construction, but he argues that his "presumption of liberty" construction is *required* by the original understanding of the Constitution. Yet if it is required by the

Constitution, how is that not merely interpretation? If this construction is required by the words and structure of the original Constitution, then it sounds to me as though Barnett is merely interpreting the words and structure of the Constitution.

Many prominent scholars continue to insist that there is a distinction between interpretation and construction – that interpretation is about discovering the *semantic content* or *linguistic meaning* of a text, and construction is the act of giving *legal effect* to that content.[3] It's certainly correct, as we've seen previously, that the text's original public meaning interacts with other legal rules in the system, and sometimes those other rules contribute to the legal effect of the text's meaning. But in my view, it does not matter too greatly whether we call that construction or just interpretation. If it's merely interpretation, then the debate between the presumption of constitutionality and the presumption of liberty, for example, is over the original meaning of the Constitution. That meaning is informed by competing theories of legitimacy that might point to either a presumption of constitutionality or a presumption of liberty. If it is a construction that we have to choose, then we still must have some *reason* for choosing one construction over the other. And that reason depends on whether you think the democratic elements or the natural rights elements predominate, or are more important, and so on. It boils down to the same thing. So let us see which of these methods, if any, we prefer.

THE PRESUMPTION OF CONSTITUTIONALITY

The presumption of constitutionality came most definitively from Supreme Court Justice Louis Brandeis, who wrote that courts ought to, "in the exercise of their discretion, refuse an injunction unless the alleged invalidity" of a legislative act is clear.[4] But this proposition predated Brandeis by many decades. He cited several famous justices, including Chief Justice John Marshall, for the proposition. Harvard law professor James Bradley Thayer had written forty years earlier, in 1893, that the Supreme Court "can only disregard [an] Act when those who have the right to make laws have not merely made a mistake, but have made a very clear one – so clear that it is not open to rational question."[5]

Robert Bork appropriated the presumption of constitutionality to originalism in his 1971 article that some claim to be originalism's intellectual birth: "In *Lochner*, Justice [Rufus W.] Peckham, defending liberty from what he conceived as a mere meddlesome interference, asked, '[A]re we all … at the mercy of legislative majorities?' The correct answer, where the Constitution does not speak, must be 'yes.'"[6] The bottom line for him was that Congress or the states may legislate freely except where the Constitution explicitly reserves a substantive right. Many originalists today continue to agree with Bork.[7]

The case Bork mentioned – *Lochner v. New York* – is the (in)famous case from 1905 in which the Supreme Court struck down a New York law limiting the number of hours that bakers were permitted to work in a day, on the grounds that it infringed the freedom to contract. Progressives and judicial minimalists attacked the decision as being antidemocratic. This case may be an example of an actual difference in outcome when using different presumptions. Progressives have charged – and here the conservative Bork agreed – that the decision violated the presumption of constitutionality. Nothing clearly prohibits the states from making such laws, and so we should assume it is constitutional even if it infringes on liberty (indeed, most laws infringe on liberty in some way). Justice Peckham and his majority in 1905, and libertarians today, would respond that the people have unenumerated liberties, including economic liberty and the liberty to contract, and legislative majorities can't simply run roughshod over them. One could say the Justices in *Lochner* applied a presumption of liberty.

Lochner shows that real differences might arise in interpreting the famously broad provisions of the Fourteenth Amendment – the Equal Protection Clause, the Due Process Clause, and the Privileges or Immunities Clause. Lino Graglia, who advocates for a presumption of constitutionality, complains most about the Court's interpretation of the Fourteenth Amendment. He argues that giving the Court such "unlimited policymaking power" through the words "due process" and "equal protection" deprives the American people "of their most important constitutional right – the right to self-government."[8] The *Lochner* majority used just these provisions to protect what it viewed as essential individual liberties.

From these arguments we see how the presumption of constitutionality might differ from the presumption of liberty: the latter, as we shall now see, would result in more democratically enacted laws struck down as violations of the Fourteenth Amendment and other rights provisions, whereas the former would result in fewer struck down.

THE PRESUMPTION OF LIBERTY

Recall that in his book *Restoring the Lost Constitution: The Presumption of Liberty*, Barnett argues that a constitution can only be legitimate if it protects our natural rights. He then argues that, when properly understood, the original meaning of the Constitution enshrines a "presumption of liberty" that puts the onus on the government to prove that its acts are necessary and proper to achieving its legitimate ends. In other words, the Constitution requires judges to presume that the people should be free of government regulation, whether state or federal, and it is up to the government to rebut this presumption. This view of constitutional legitimacy and of our Constitution's original meaning is shared by many libertarian law professors and practitioners, such as Timothy Sandefur of the Pacific Legal Foundation,[9] Chip Mellor of the Institute for Justice,[10] and the prolific Richard Epstein, previously of the University of Chicago and currently of NYU Law School.[11]

Barnett explains that the text itself points to the presumption of liberty. He argues that, when properly understood, the Commerce Clause, the Necessary and Proper Clause, the Ninth Amendment, and the Privileges or Immunities Clause of the Fourteenth Amendment all enshrine this presumption. "The original meaning of these nearly lost clauses," he writes, "argues strongly against a presumption of constitutionality and in favor of the contrary construction ...: the Presumption of Liberty."[12] The gist of this presumption is that it "would place the burden on the government to show why its interference with liberty is both necessary and proper rather than ... imposing a burden on the citizen to show why the exercise of a particular liberty is a 'fundamental right.'"[13]

Now of course that makes at least some textual sense. The Ninth Amendment does state, "The enumeration in the Constitution, of certain rights, shall not be construed to deny or disparage others retained by the people." Why should we presume an act to be constitutional just because it does not violate a right clearly expressed elsewhere in the Constitution (usually in the Bill of Rights), as the conservatives would have it? Wouldn't that render the Ninth Amendment meaningless? Isn't is just as plausible – or even more plausible – that we should presume the act to be *un*constitutional because it might violate those other rights "retained by the people" but not explicitly spelled out in the Constitution?

Further, the Necessary and Proper Clause (also known as the "Elastic Clause" or the "Sweeping Clause" for obvious reasons), which has been one of the key justifications for the dramatic expansion of federal power over the last century, states: "The Congress shall have Power To ... make all Laws which shall be necessary and proper for carrying into Execution the foregoing Powers." By "foregoing powers" the text is referring to the specific and limited enumeration of federal power in article I, section 8 of the Constitution. Now, we often think of that clause as only requiring legislation "necessary" for exercising those other powers. But Barnett argues that the legislation also has to be "proper," which, he argues, means that it cannot violate preexisting, unenumerated rights.

So the presumption of liberty, in my view, is a quite plausible interpretation of the Constitution. There are two takeaways. First, this interpretation seems equally plausible to the presumption of constitutionality. Second, it's not at all clear why Barnett considers the presumption of liberty (or the presumption of constitutionality) to be a "construction." If the Ninth Amendment and the Necessary and Proper Clause require the presumption of liberty as a matter of interpretation, then it's just that – interpretation.

Now, on this second point, other libertarian thinkers do suggest more firmly that this kind of presumption would be a construction. In *The Classical Liberal Constitution*, Epstein admits that the constitutional text is vague and we must therefore interpret it with particular background principles. He claims that classical liberalism (which is more or less consistent with modern-day libertarianism) is the proper choice for interpretation, because it was the most significant moral theory at work during the Founding era. Epstein writes: "In its enduring provisions, our Constitution is most emphatically a classical liberal document. Its successful interpretation on all points dealing with text and its surrounding norms should be read in sync with the tradition of strong property rights, voluntary association, and limited government."[14]

Epstein makes the argument that we should therefore adopt a kind of presumption of classical liberalism – a presumption of economic liberty, and liberty more generally – because the Founders assumed that theory as a starting point. But of course, we recall from the previous chapter that the Founders also believed that the Constitution had to be democratic to be legitimate. Classical liberalism itself, which does not actually require democracy, was not the only moral theory at work during the Founding Era. Republicanism and democratic theory were as well.

ORIGINAL INTERPRETIVE CONVENTIONS

There is another view, and one that I find more persuasive than other theories of construction. There has been some recent scholarship on what have been referred to as *original interpretive conventions*. These include not only, say, the rules of grammar and syntax that existed at the time of the Founding but also other rules that were used to interpret legal documents. For example, certain phrases had "technical" meanings whereas others were to be interpreted with "plain" meaning. The rule against superfluity – the idea that it is incorrect to interpret one provision in such a way as to make another provision superfluous – was another interpretive convention.

Law professors John McGinnis and Michael Rappaport claim that nothing from the Founding era suggests that that generation saw a distinction between interpretation and construction. They therefore suggest that construction may not be necessary at all – that the Constitution, when interpreted using original interpretive conventions, will always come up with a most probable answer.[15] That last part is key: we don't have to be one hundred percent certain. All knowledge is probabilistic. And, they argue, when evidence cuts both ways after deploying all interpretive tools available, it was understood that the interpretation more strongly supported by the evidence would prevail.[16]

But even this theory might be unable entirely to avoid the debate between the presumption of liberty and the presumption of constitutionality, for two reasons. First, it is highly unlikely that interpretive tools will *always* give us the certainty we desire when making constitutional decisions. Indeed, Caleb Nelson has written that there was at least some uncertainty in the Founding generation as to the interpretive conventions applicable to the Constitution.[17] Justice Joseph Story, one of the great jurists of the nineteenth century, argued in 1833 that much of the difficulty in constitutional law in the first four decades "had its origin in the want of some uniform rules of interpretation."[18]

In other words, original interpretive conventions – the rules of grammar and syntax, the rule against superfluities, the rule against absurdities, other legal rules in the system bearing on interpretation – might go a long way in helping us determine the original meaning (or legal effect) of a constitutional provision in a particular context. Indeed, I think original meaning as given effect by these original interpretive conventions can provide most of the answers we seek to historical legal questions. But even these might not answer *every* question.

Second, and more importantly, the presumption of liberty and the presumption of constitutionality might have been a *part* of the original interpretive conventions of the Founding generation. It may be that interpreters were expected to deploy various interpretive conventions, but then the answer to the constitutional question might still appear uncertain; either outcome might seem equally plausible. At the time of the Founding, there appears to have been some disagreement over whether a "tie-breaking" interpretive convention like the presumption of liberty, or a different tie-breaking interpretive convention like the presumption of constitutionality, should apply in those close cases where original meaning and all the other interpretive conventions did not lead to a definitive answer.

For example, at least two leading luminaries from the Founding generation advocated something like a presumption of liberty. St. George Tucker explained that the Constitution ought to receive a "strict construction, wherever the right of personal liberty, of personal security, or of private property may become the subject of dispute."[19] And Thomas Jefferson famously advocated against a "broad construction" of the Constitution in favor of a "rigorous construction": "I had rather ask an enlargement of power from the nation [through constitutional amendments]," he wrote, "than to assume it by a construction which would make our powers boundless."[20]

On the other hand, Chief Justice Marshall famously rejected "strict construction" in favor of reading constitutional provisions according to "their natural and obvious import," "as fairly understood," and in their "natural sense."[21] Story agreed, claiming that constitutional questions should depend "upon a fair construction of the whole instrument."[22,*] Rappaport and McGinnis have suggested that, after the usual interpretive tools were used to determine the proper and fair construction, a presumption of constitutionality as a last resort was part of the interpretive conventions existing at the time of the Founding.[23] And McGinnis, in a separate article, argues that judges had a "duty" as part of the judicial power to "clarify" the meaning of a law before striking it down as unconstitutional or upholding its constitutionality. He canvasses numerous examples of jurists from the Founding period who, in exercise of that judicial duty, clarified the meaning of the Constitution using the accepted interpretive conventions of the time but who then would only strike down a statute if its clarified meaning was a "clear" violation of the Constitution.[24]

THE NATURE OF THE CONSTITUTION

So which of these two tie-breaking interpretive conventions (and there may be others out there) we adopt in close cases, where the answer is still indeterminate, remains an open question even as a matter of originalist methods. For what it is worth, almost all federal judges rely on some variant of the presumption of constitutionality

---

* Note that all of these authors use the term "construction," but their use suggests that they did not see a distinction between interpretation and construction. Indeed, where Story discusses these interpretive methods in his *Commentaries*, he uses the terms "strict interpretation" and "large interpretation," rather than strict and broad construction. JOSEPH STORY, I COMMENTARIES ON THE CONSTITUTION OF THE UNITED STATES 385–86 (Forgotten Books 2015) (1833).

and most academics agree with it as well. Very few adhere to or advocate a presumption of liberty.

My view is that it is not obvious that the Constitution requires one or the other. All originalists agree that to interpret the Constitution, we at a minimum must consider the purposes and structure of the Constitution, just as we consider the purposes and structure of statutes. William Blackstone taught that "the most universal and effectual way of discovering the true meaning of a law, when the words are dubious, is by considering the *reason* and *spirit* of it; or the cause which moved the legislator to enact it."[25] Story then taught:

> In construing the constitution of the United States, we are, in the first instance, to consider what are its nature and objects, its scope and design, as apparent from the structure of the instrument, viewed as a whole, and also viewed in its component parts. ... Where the words admit of two senses, each of which is conformable to common usage, that sense it to be adopted, which, without departing from the literal import of the words, best harmonizes with the nature and objects, the scope and design of the instrument.[26]

But as we have seen, the nature and object, the scope and design of the Constitution are multifaceted. On the one hand it was intended to enable democratic government, on the other to protect liberty. It was intended to create an effective national government, but one of only enumerated powers. It was intended to preserve a large measure of state sovereignty, but also individual rights. These interests, as we have seen, are often competing. In my view, then, it is not clear which "construction" or "tie-breaking interpretation" is the better one. It seems to me that different contexts might require use of one or the other. Which of these interpretive conventions, in what contexts, is the best interpretive choice may be one of the greatest unresolved questions in originalism.

LIQUIDATION: FIXING CONSTITUTIONAL MEANING

So what should be done in those hard cases where interpretation truly "runs out"? What do we do when we've used all our interpretive rules and canons and the constitutional answer still isn't clear? If there's no intelligible way to decide between the presumption of constitutionality or the presumption of liberty, is there nothing more we can do? I think there is more we can do. Or at least, we can settle on a second-best option. The first few times a judge or other constitutional actor makes a choice as to what a truly ambiguous constitutional provision means, it will in some sense be an arbitrary choice among the competing plausible options. But after it has been decided – preferably over the course of a *series* of mature deliberations made by many constitutional actors – future cases within that same context will presumably accord such collective decisions determinative weight and the matter will be settled.

That's how some of our most prominent Founders expected interpretation to happen. The reader might now recall the earlier discussion of *Federalist* No. 37. James Madison understood that language was ambiguous and indeterminate; he thought that particular discussions and adjudications would "liquidate," or "fix," the meaning of otherwise indeterminate provisions.[27] Thus, the question whether the president had power to remove principal officers without Senate consent, or whether the Necessary and Proper clause authorized a Bank of the United States, may have been open questions at the time of ratification. But the great debates in both Congress and the Executive resolving these questions (in favor of the president's unitary power of removal, and in favor of a Bank of the United States) was understood to "fix" the meaning of the relevant constitutional provisions.

In Representative Madison's words, Congress's interpretation of the removal power would become a "permanent exposition of the constitution."[28] Although he had opposed the First Bank of the United States, he refused to veto the Second Bank of the United States as president on constitutional grounds. His prior constitutional objection, he wrote, was "precluded ... by repeated recognitions under varied circumstances of the validity of such an institution in the acts of the legislative, executive, and judicial branches of the Government, accompanied by indications ... of a concurrence of the general will of the nation."[29]

When President Washington inquired of the Senate whether it believed an Indian treaty required ratification, Washington stated "that this point should be well considered and settled, so that our national proceedings, in this respect, may become uniform, and be directed by

fixed and stable principles."[30] And when the question of the constitutionality of the 1789 Judiciary Act's requirement that Supreme Court
Justices ride circuit (that is, travel across the country to hear appeals)
came before the Supreme Court, the Justices declared that "practice
and acquiescence under it for a period of several years, commencing
with the organization of the judicial system, affords an irresistible
answer, and has indeed fixed the construction."[31]

In the same way that through practice and precedent the meaning
of a provision can become liquidated, so too can the relevant interpretive conventions – such as the presumption of constitutionality, for
example – become liquidated. To take a different example, it was an
open question at the time of the founding whether the Ex Post Facto
Clause should be interpreted by its plain meaning to prohibit all
retrospective legislation, or by its technical meaning to prohibit only
retrospective criminal laws. Early interpretations settled on the technical and thus helped "fix" or "liquidate" the idea that at least this
provision of the Constitution should be read in its technical sense.[32]
There may be some indeterminacy in choosing interpretive conventions (such as one of our presumptions), but, once the conventions
have been deployed, their use in particular contexts can also be fixed
from then on.

This ultimate interpretive convention – that of liquidating and
fixing indeterminate meaning – was thus the most important convention
of them all. Even if originalism with all its other original interpretive
conventions at its disposal still does not answer every question – even if it
can only narrow down the range of plausible interpretations – we still
have a way forward. The wheels of our constitutional system do not grind
to a halt. The Congress, the president, the courts, and even the people
themselves were expected to debate on important constitutional ambiguities. Once those debates are settled – so long as they can plausibly be said
to have been truly settled over the course of a series of deliberations
among multiple constitutional actors[33] – then we will have our answer.
The Constitution's meaning, even if originally indeterminate, will have
become fixed for us by subsequent discussions and adjudications.

Such an interpretive system may not be perfect. It may not answer
all questions. But it answers many questions. And really, it's not such a
bad way of doing things.

PART III

Objections and Recapitulation

6   LAWYERS AS HISTORIANS

"There are many objective truths to be told about the past –
great and vital truths that are relevant and even urgent to the
needs of mankind."[1]

David Hackett Fischer, Historians' Fallacies (1970)

Nonoriginalists often claim that originalism is impractical because
it requires lawyers to be historians. What do lawyers know about
doing history, and who's to say they'll be any good at it? Often history
is complex, so the argument goes, and does not offer any definitive
answers. Further – and here we get to the most potent criticism of
using history – historical knowledge is all relative, so we can't obtain
any "true" historical answers anyway.

The aim of this chapter is to challenge such notions.[2] It will show
that lawyers can be good historians – at least, they can be as good as
professional historians. It will show that the skills necessary to do good
history are the same skills that lawyers must use every day. It will also
show that historical knowledge, even if it is sometimes uncertain or
indeterminate, can still be useful for legal analysis.

At bottom, originalists rarely claim that there will be one right
historical answer for every legal question requiring historical analysis.
What they do claim is that some legal questions to which originalism
is relevant admit of only one answer, and that many others admit
of a *circumscribed range* of possible answers. Originalism may not
always offer one clearly correct historical answer, but it might still
disprove prevailing nonoriginalist interpretations of certain constitutional provisions.

IS HISTORY TOO HARD?

Lawyers aren't historians. So who's to say lawyers would be any good
at doing history? Unearthing historical answers is hard work, and
sometimes there might not be enough evidence for us to know what
was really going on. David Strauss has regularly criticized originalism,
and he relies heavily on this notion that lawyers aren't historians:

> On the most practical level, it is often impossible to uncover what
> the original understandings were: what people thought they were
> doing when they adopted the various provisions of the Constitu-
> tion. Discovering how people in the past thought about their world
> is the task of historians, and there is no reason to think that lawyers
> and judges are going to be good at doing that kind of history –
> especially when they are dealing with controversial legal issues that
> arouse strong sentiments.[3]

Elsewhere he has added that

> the originalist project [is] a particularly difficult, challenging form
> of intellectual history and one that often will, to the honest origin-
> alist, turn up the answer "I don't know," or "there were various
> ideas and none clearly prevailed," or "they were just confused back
> then." That is one difficulty with originalism. Too often, it will be
> just too hard to figure out the answers to the relevant historical
> questions.[4]

I think we can tease out three criticisms here: historians are better at
doing history; legal issues are so controversial that dispassionate analysis is difficult; and history often fails to provide us with determinate
answers.

Regarding the last two of these criticisms, they seem flawed because
they are not unique to originalism. Surely it is true that history is more
difficult to do objectively when dealing with "controversial legal issues
that arouse strong sentiments." But many purely historical questions
are also controversial and arouse strong sentiments. Did the Reagan
administration's policies vis-à-vis right-wing dictatorships enable gross
violations of human rights or ultimately promote the cause of freedom
by preventing communist insurgencies? Was the civil war fought to
perpetuate the union, abolish slavery, or line the pockets of greedy

Lawyers as Historians   101

northern industrialists? Conversely, even nonhistorical legal questions are controversial and arouse strong sentiments – consider the abortion or gay marriage cases – yet surely that does not mean lawyers shouldn't do law.

True, lawyers may be prone to using selective evidence in favor of their clients. But a judge will get briefs from both sides. Plus, historians themselves routinely approach controversial historical topics with ideological agendas. Yet we don't give up the study of human rights policies, the roots of slavery, and other such topics for that reason. It is just as easy (or hard) to answer a legal history question as it is to answer any other historical question from the relevant period. Historical questions might be controversial, or disputed, or have an uncertain answer, but at minimum we may be able to learn a circumscribed range of things that may turn out to be quite useful.

ARE HISTORIANS REALLY BETTER AT HISTORY THAN LAWYERS?

What about David Strauss's other claim, that we should leave history to the historians? I should first like to point out that this criticism might be said of *any* tool a lawyer might employ to solve legal questions. Lawyers are not historians, to be sure; but neither are they linguists, philosophers, sociologists, or economists. Language will have indeterminacies, people disagree over philosophy, and one can find droves of economists on opposite sides of any particular question. Yet nonoriginalism routinely asks of lawyers that they be moral philosophers, sociologists, or economists – not to mention that any legal theory at minimum requires lawyers to be linguists of a sort. If history is deemed relevant for constitutional interpretation because the historical understanding is, for whatever reason, legitimate, then history is no worse a tool to use in legal analysis than economics, linguistics, or moral philosophy.

What is more, even professional historians who decry the perversions of "law office history" commit the very same errors they accuse us non-historian lawyers of committing. The historian David Hackett Fischer, in his celebrated book *Historians' Fallacies*,[5] cataloged and described more than one hundred fallacies common in historical literature. These are fallacies committed by professional historians almost too numerous to count. Yet no one suggests that historians should not do history. Rather, they must do it better.

Indeed, professional historians have even committed these fallacies in their amicus briefs submitted to the Supreme Court. The interested reader may consult a past law review article of mine for some humorous examples.[6] For present purposes, my point is that there is no reason that history must be particularly difficult for lawyers, as opposed to others, to do. Indeed, I think lawyers and judges are particularly well suited to do history. A trial judge, for example, must routinely assess various accounts and testimony, weigh credibility given different motives and backgrounds, and come to a conclusion about something that transpired in the past. That is exactly what historians must do.

Consider also that many perfectly typical legal questions require lawyers to do similar kinds of history. As Stephen Sachs has written, "*Nemo dat* might require us to figure out whether *A* or *B* owned Blackacre long ago. State border disputes can turn on the proper construction of an old interstate compact or the Crown grant to Lord Baltimore. Ex post facto claims force courts to determine what the law was when a crime was committed, not what it is today. And so on."[7] But no one argues that lawyers shouldn't do history in those contexts.

IS HISTORICAL TRUTH POSSIBLE?

Finally, perhaps a more interesting attack on the use of history is the claim that there's no such thing as objective historical knowledge at all. This notion is rooted in two philosophical innovations of the nineteenth and twentieth centuries: historicism and relativism. Historicism is the school in the philosophy of history that denies transcendental truth; all truths and values are relative to their historical time and place.

In a nutshell, the historicist criticism of originalism consists in the following notion: we cannot operate without modern presuppositions, and so we can never obtain objective or useful historical knowledge. The originalist enterprise is therefore impossible. The historicist criticism can take at least two forms. First, it can take the form of the proposition that historical knowledge may be true and "objective" but only relative to its particular time and place. Second, it can take the form of the proposition that no objective knowledge is possible at all.

Historicism first influenced constitutional scholarship in the mid-twentieth century. Many scholars believed "that properly conducted historical inquiry illuminated only the past and was thus irrelevant to contemporary social issues." But the knowledge we could have about the past was still "objective," investigated by a "disinterested" "scientific investigator."[8] In other words, history can reveal objective truths, but these "truths" are only objective *relative* to a time and place; they tell us nothing enduring. That is how the famous twentieth-century political philosopher Leo Strauss described historicism: historicists tried "to discover standards which, while being objective, were relative to particular historical situations."[9]

Even if this version of historicism were correct, originalism overcomes it. If we are originalists, we only care about the historical truth of one particular time and place: America from 1787 to 1789. Thus even if historical knowledge is only objective relative to a particular time and place, the very inquiry in originalist analysis is to determine the objective historical knowledge relative to the Founders' time and place.

There is a slight variation of historicism, however, that would be lethal to originalism as a constitutional theory if it were not wrong. It is the idea that all modern people, including modern lawyers, are unable truly to understand any historical thought because we cannot escape our modern presuppositions. (Note, of course, that this argument applies to everyone, including historians themselves!) The argument goes as follows. All modern people have assumptions, presuppositions, preconceived notions, and the like, and these *always* affect how we interpret historical facts. Put more academically, "these models and preconceptions in terms of which we unavoidably organize and adjust our perceptions and thoughts will themselves tend to act as determinants of what we think or perceive."[10]

That means when we want to make an historical conclusion based on some historical evidence, that conclusion will be tainted by our particular assumptions and presuppositions. We cannot attain actual historical knowledge, only our own particular gloss on past historical facts. We can only give *present* meaning to *past* facts. "The perpetual danger, in our attempts to enlarge our historical understanding, is thus that our expectations about what someone must be saying or doing will themselves determine that we understand the agent to be doing something which he would not – or even could not – himself have accepted as an account of what he *was* doing."[11]

This epistemological problem is often conceived in terms of "translation." One legal scholar has described the problem thus: as the historian "renders the past meaningful in the present, [he] cannot avoid changing its meaning, just as the Egyptologist who translates hieroglyphics into English through Greek can at best only approximate their original meaning."[12] The change that the historian begets depends on his particular point of view. "A...historian selects one historical interpretation in preference to another on the basis of its consistency with his own value system or world view, or that of his audience."[13]

Both of these versions of historicism have elements of relativism. But relativist historicism is a flawed idea for a number of reasons. First, no matter from what perspective one approaches history, *some* facts are simply true from all perspectives. Indeed, common sense suggests that historicism is wrong in at least some obvious circumstances relevant to originalism. For example, the Eleventh Amendment, whatever else it might mean, at minimum overturned *Chisholm v. Georgia*. The Establishment Clause, whatever else it might mean, at minimum means that there is to be no official church and no religious taxation. The freedom of speech, whatever else it might mean, does not protect private parties from libel suits. None of these points can be known without the historical background of the Constitution's or the amendments' framings.

The most critical reason why historicism is flawed, however, is that it is self-contradictory. If all knowledge is relative to a particular time and place, and has no objective value beyond the partial perspective and presuppositions of the particular individual, then isn't *historicism itself* merely one "perspective" unique to the cultural, intellectual, and historical context of its proponents? As Leo Strauss, a prominent political theorist of the last century, has written,

> The historicist thesis is ... exposed to a very obvious difficulty which cannot be solved but only evaded or obscured by considerations of a

> more subtle character. Historicism asserts that all human thoughts or beliefs are historical, and hence deservedly destined to perish; but historicism itself is a human thought; hence historicism can be of only temporary validity, or it cannot be simply true. To assert the historicist thesis means to doubt it and thus to transcend it.... Historicism thrives on the fact that it inconsistently exempts itself from its own verdict about all human thought. The historicist thesis is self-contradictory or absurd. We cannot see the historical character of "all" thought – that is, of all thought with the exception of the historicist insight and its implications – without transcending history, without grasping something trans-historical.[14]

In other words, historicism is itself merely a historical thought that is not always true. Or it proves that there is at least one historical truth (historicism), and then it becomes a matter of finding out what other historical truths are out there.

There are other commonsense reasons why historicism seems flawed. Consider that we *also* have different presuppositions from person to person within a time and place, or within merely a short span of time, and so forth. Even next-door neighbors have had different life experiences and often have different assumptions and presuppositions. Does that mean communication, or obtaining shared knowledge, is impossible?

We can return to the translation metaphor: recall that historicists claimed that history is "lost in translation," so to speak, in the same way that some of the meaning of the original hieroglyphics was lost when translated indirectly from the Greek. But that notion is somewhat silly: even if we had translated hieroglyphics *directly* into English, *any* translation into another language will only approximate the original meaning. Does that mean that a Frenchman and an American can never understand one another?

That's not to say differences in background don't exist. It's only to say that despite differences, objective human knowledge might be, and likely is, possible. Otherwise communication between any two human beings would be impossible. To say, then, that objective historical knowledge is impossible is to say also that *all* knowledge is impossible. If that were true, then any other legal method would be just as arbitrary as an originalist one because it would rely on some other knowledge that is still subjective. And you may as well stop wasting your time with this book – and any other book too – because it is impossible for us to understand one another.

RECAPITULATION

In this chapter, we have encountered three broad criticisms of originalism's use of history. First, we encountered the objection that historical evidence will often pull in different directions, that there might not be one right answer, and that historical evidence may be too scant to draw legal conclusions. To this an originalist would say, "Why, of course that's true! But also beside the point." Let us assume that history can resolve at least *some* questions. Originalists believe that the original understanding of the Constitution, as elucidated by the historical materials, should be determinative in those cases. Originalists also understand that the historical materials may suggest a range of possible answers, but that range will often be circumscribed enough to refute certain nonoriginalist interpretations. Finally, originalists understand that in some cases, the historical evidence may be truly indeterminate. In *that* case, originalists concede that something else must govern (for example, perhaps the presumption of constitutionality directs the outcome in such cases). But those cases are few and far between and cannot justify abandoning history at all times.

Second, we encountered the objection that lawyers just aren't good at doing history. But the criticisms launched against lawyers doing history can just as easily apply to lawyers doing anything else – economics, linguistics, sociology, philosophy – and yet nonoriginalists rarely criticize themselves for engaging in *those* disciplines, which they do frequently. Further, the errors allegedly committed by "law office historians" are similar to the errors frequently committed by professional historians. Both lawyers and professional historians need to avoid such errors, but it's just a matter of learning the proper tools. And indeed, lawyers and judges who must routinely weigh credibility and assess evidence about past events may be particularly well suited to do history.

Third, some claim that historical knowledge isn't possible at all or that we cannot avoid mistranslating past facts into present meaning. But even if this objection were true, it would apply to all human knowledge at all times. Therefore, using history would be no better or worse than using any other method for interpreting the Constitution. Moreover, our common experience belies these objections. Of course we always have to be aware of preconceptions and, in historical studies, strive to understand past people as they understood themselves. Just because the task isn't easy does not mean it's impossible. But if *some* knowledge weren't possible, then neither would be human communication or progress of any kind.

7 *BROWN V. BOARD* AND ORIGINALISM

> "*Brown* is a fixed point in constitutional law; no approach to
> constitutional interpretation can survive if it does not accept
> *Brown*."[1]
>
> *David Strauss (2012)*

Nonoriginalists often claim that originalism must fail as a constitutional theory because it cannot justify *Brown v. Board of Education*, the famous 1955 Supreme Court case rejecting the "separate but equal" doctrine and mandating the desegregation of schools. A friend once told me that any method of constitutional interpretation that cannot justify *Brown* has an uphill battle for acceptance. I responded to my friend that originalism *can* justify *Brown*, and in this chapter we shall see how.

Before making the case, I'd like to remind the reader that my friend's comment, as well as the David Strauss quotation used as this chapter's epigraph, gets it backward. Remember, a proper originalist must first decide what the Constitution in fact *says*; only then can he or she ask whether the Constitution is just and worthy of obedience. It may be that originalism cannot justify *Brown*. In that case, we may have to abandon the Constitution. Perhaps a prosegregation outcome in *Brown* would have justified open revolt. The point is only that it is exceedingly dangerous to conflate interpretation and legitimacy, to ask what the Constitution *must* say before investigating what it *does* say. That is a sure way to get wrong answers. Many originalists have fallen into this trap as well, but that is a subject for another time.

I acknowledge that this argument isn't too satisfying in the context of *Brown*. Desegregation involves so fundamental a principle that we really should hope that our Constitution requires it. So let us see how originalists justify *Brown*. There is a vast literature on this case, and I cannot do justice to all the different views. Older originalists rejected *Brown*, though one would be hard-pressed to find many today who still do. Their reasoning was rooted in the claim that the Congress that enacted and ratified the Fourteenth Amendment, with its Equal Protection Clause and Privileges or Immunities Clause, did not think that it would apply to school desegregation. After all, the same Congress that wrote the Fourteenth Amendment continued to segregate schools in the District of Columbia, over which it had direct legislative responsibility.

How could Congress have thought the Fourteenth Amendment applied to desegregation if it continued to segregate? This view highlights an original expected applications approach that we have already rejected. But we must not reject this position out of hand. Just because most originalists do not adopt an original expected applications approach does not mean *Brown* necessarily can be justified under other theories of originalism. Clearly, how the Congress thought the language of the Fourteenth Amendment would apply is significant evidence of the *meaning* of the amendment's words.

There are generally two approaches to justifying *Brown* that highlight different elements in originalist thinking and will help us review everything we have learned thus far. The first view we will explore is the one advanced by Michael McConnell in his famous *Virginia Law Review* article on this subject.

McConnell argues that significant historical evidence suggests that many of the framers of the Fourteenth Amendment in Congress in the 1860s (and a bit later, in the 1870s) *did* think it would apply to school desegregation. Or at least there is sufficient competing evidence to make the holding in *Brown* within the plausible range of originalist meanings of the Fourteenth Amendment. When we explore McConnell's position, we can thus review a bit the role of history in originalism and how we might apply historical evidence to constitutional questions. *Brown* is a good case study in the application of the use of history.

The second approach was advanced in a crude form by Robert Bork and, I think, perfected by Christopher Green in his article on the sense-reference distinction, which we briefly touched on in the chapter on the "meaning of meaning." The basic idea is that the words of the Equal Protection Clause (or, some would say, the Privileges or Immunities Clause) of the Fourteenth Amendment enact a principle, and how that principle applies to certain *facts* may change over time as we learn more about the facts. Perhaps the framers and ratifiers were wrong about the facts, and thus about how the principle should be applied to that circumstance. Green would say that the Privileges or Immunities Clause had a sense, and its real-world referent cannot depend on factual mistakes or erroneous understandings as to how that sense functions in the world.

Indeed, it could very well be that the framers of the Fourteenth Amendment *knew* or *suspected* that the principle they were enshrining was inconsistent with the segregation then existing. Just because the Founders owned slaves did not mean they thought that their principle that "all men are created equal" applied only to white men. The letters and writings of the Founders make clear that they all thought slavery inconsistent with that great principle, but they owned that they could not resolve this inconsistency in their lifetimes. Perhaps something similar occurred with desegregation and the Fourteenth Amendment.

In my view, both of these positions make sense, and they really work in tandem to make a persuasive case for *Brown*. Ultimately, if absolutely no one at the time thought that the sense of the Fourteenth Amendment would require desegregation, it would be exceedingly difficult to argue that the referent could change over time. Perhaps the facts did change – perhaps we did come to learn that separate was inherently unequal – but could the framers of the Fourteenth Amendment have been 100 percent ignorant of the relevant facts? It is hard to imagine. Not impossible to imagine, but hard. So long as there was a vibrant debate over the application at the time, which serves as evidence to us about the sense of the words used, it is possible to conclude that the real-world referent of the sense changed as we came better to understand the relevant facts.

MICHAEL MCCONNELL AND HISTORICAL EVIDENCE

McConnell explains that the claim that the framers and ratifiers of the Fourteenth Amendment did not think it would desegregate schools hinges on two key pieces of evidence: first, that segregation continued to exist in DC, over which Congress had legislative authority; and second, that the preratification discussions of the Fourteenth Amendment from 1866 to 1868 contained only a few ambiguous statements about desegregation.[2] The problem with the DC segregation argument is that segregation in the public schools there already *existed*; the Congress that acted upon the Fourteenth Amendment never took *affirmative* actions to create segregated schools in DC in this period. The fact of continuing segregation is thus little evidence of what they thought about it.[3]

The problem with the second argument is that the fact that few people *were* talking about an issue is very little evidence of how many at the time *would have* thought about it. McConnell's key project is to look at the evidence from immediately *after* the ratification of the Fourteenth Amendment. Once it was enacted, how did Congress think it would apply? It turns out there was significant discussion of school desegregation when the Civil Rights Act of 1875, which at one point would have desegregated schools and other public accommodations, was debated between 1872 and 1875.

McConnell persuasively shows that a significant majority of both houses of Congress thought that the Fourteenth Amendment required school desegregation. At one point, the Republicans in Congress who were advancing the bill and who opposed segregation garnered almost two-thirds support in both chambers. But they were two votes shy of the mark, and procedural rules then existing in the House required a two-thirds vote to overcome filibusters and other delaying tactics. The Republicans never got their filibuster-proof two-thirds supermajority.[4]

Not only did large majorities in both chambers of Congress support desegregation, but majorities in both also voted *down* the statutory amendments to enshrine "separate but equal" into law. After the Democrats won a landslide victory in the 1874 elections, the Republicans could only get a civil rights bill passed that included separate but equal. Instead of enshrining this "invidious discrimination in the laws of this country," they opted for a civil rights bill without any language on public schools at all.[5]

McConnell explains the implications of this evidence for originalism and *Brown v. Board*:

> A close examination of the debates and votes on segregation
> between 1870 and 1875 now convinces me that *Brown v. Board
> of Education* was correctly decided on originalist grounds, not on
> the basis of any high level of generality about equality, but on
> the basis of the actual discussions and understandings of school
> segregation in the period immediately following ratification of
> the Amendment. At a minimum, history shows that the position
> adopted by the Court in *Brown* was within the legitimate range of
> interpretations commonly held at the time.[6]

This summation reminds us how we might use conflicting historical
evidence. Conflicting evidence may still reveal a range of plausible
originalist meanings. The question, of course, remains: How does a
court then decide among these plausible meanings?

McConnell believes we should look to the preponderance of the
evidence. In other words, he hedges when he states that, at minimum,
Brown's holding was within the range of plausible meaning. He actually
thinks that *Brown*'s holding is in fact the *best* answer, given the available
evidence. It is the most probable conclusion given the near-supermajority
support for that interpretation in Congress in the early 1870s.[7]

The reader interested in exploring McConnell's argument in
full should also consult Michael Klarman's response to McConnell,[8]
and McConnell's reply.[9] I shall briefly summarize this debate here,
only because it reveals some common misperceptions about originalism. Klarman finds three main theoretical faults with McConnell's
reasoning. Klarman first argues that "[i]t is inconceivable that most –
indeed even very many – Americans in 1866–68 would have endorsed
a constitutional amendment to forbid public school segregation." But
that is hardly the question for originalists. Whether a separate amendment specifically banning public school segregation would have been
enacted is immaterial to the question of whether the broader amendment that was enacted includes such a prohibition; similarly, it does not
matter what the ratifying public would have thought had it considered
the particular question at hand. As McConnell explains, there is almost
no discussion of the issue of desegregation at all in the debates over
ratification of the Fourteenth Amendment. The serious discussion of
the issue first came a few years later, during the debates over the Civil
Rights Act of 1875. The question is not what the public would have

thought in 1868, had it thought at all about the issue; the question is rather what the public in fact enacted and whether that required desegregation. And the first serious debate over whether the as-enacted Fourteenth Amendment required a prohibition of segregation suggests that those tasked with interpreting the amendment believed that it did. That is entitled to significant weight. Klarman's argument that McConnell focuses too much on 1872–75 rather than 1866 falls flat for this same reason.

Klarman's remaining argument is that McConnell never justified his preference for the views of the congressional interpreters during the Civil Rights Act debates over the views of the public that appeared adamantly opposed to desegregation. Here the same problem arises: the public may have been opposed to desegregation, but there is almost no evidence that the public gave much thought at all to the implications for that preference of the Fourteenth Amendment it was enacting. The congressional debates in 1872–75, on the other hand, reflected what individuals *actually engaging in acts of interpretation* believed the amendment required.

Indeed, McConnell nicely rebuts Klarman's points by pointing out that, by his reasoning, the Fifteenth Amendment's guaranteeing the right of blacks to vote doesn't actually guarantee them the right to vote. After all, much of the public at the time opposed black voting rights, and it took decades for the Fifteenth Amendment to be fully implemented. Surely that has little bearing on what the Fifteenth Amendment actually means. As McConnell explained, "Actual practice is no surer a guide than popular opinion. It takes time for changes in the law to be fully implemented." What matters at the end of the day is what the framers and ratifiers ultimately enacted – and McConnell persuasively shows that those tasked with enforcing the amendment believed it required the desegregation of public schools.[10]

SENSE-REFERENCE AND CHANGING FACTS

I find McConnell's historical evidence persuasive. But what if we couldn't be sure which view preponderated based on the available evidence? What if you think Klarman has the better of the argument?

We might then resort to the sense-reference distinction – essentially the distinction between meaning and application – to demonstrate that *Brown* was right anyway. Robert Bork made a crude form of this argument when he explained that the principle of the Fourteenth Amendment does not change, but its application to facts can change as we come to learn more about the relevant facts. He argued that, although it may have been thought in the late 1800s that "separate" could be equal, we have come to learn as a sociological fact that separate is always unequal.[11] That argument is similar to the Supreme Court's in *Brown* – the Court relied on sociological data to show that separate was unequal as a matter of fact. But surely that's a bit unsatisfying. Even if the results showed just as good results for black children in all-black schools as for white children in all-white schools, wouldn't we think there was still something inherently unequal about segregation?

I think the sense-reference distinction clarifies the issue. Christopher Green, whose article on the sense-reference distinction was introduced in an earlier chapter, explains how the distinction serves to justify the desegregation decision *even if* the preponderance of the evidence from the 1800s was that segregation would be acceptable under the Fourteenth Amendment.

The basic idea is that the framers and ratifiers of the amendment could always get facts wrong. For example, the Framers of the Constitution hypothetically could have passed a scheme for apportionment thinking that New Jersey had a bigger population than New York and thus would get more representatives. If, after the census, it transpired that New York had a larger population, surely that would not have meant that the original expected application of the apportionment provision prevailed. New Jersey wouldn't get more representatives merely because the Framers *thought* that was how things would play out given the law they were writing.

In short, we are not bound by their factual errors. And to determine whether a factual error existed also depends on the *reasons* the proponents of a particular view gave. If a view of how a sense will function in the real world is reasonable, that is good evidence that this sense is correct. But if the reasons are very unreasonable, surely how they thought the words would function is not very good evidence of the sense of the words.

Green argues that the reasons given by the desegregation proponents in the 1870s were far more persuasive as a textual matter than
the reasons given by its opponents. Indeed, Green relies on McConnell
to show that the reasons Democrats offered in opposition were down-
right contradictory. On the one hand, they argued that segregation
was formally equal, but on the other, they charged that desegregation
would enforce *social* rather than *civil* equality – which implies that they
understood segregation to be inherently unequal.[12]

For Green, then, it doesn't matter ultimately which view predomin-
ated. What matters more is the *reasoning* about the facts behind each
view because only *that* is evidence of the true "sense" of the words. He
writes: "It is obviously more important that [Senator Charles] Sum-
ner's reasoning regarding the manner in which the social meaning of
segregation abridges civil rights, and therefore violates the Fourteenth
Amendment, is persuasive than that it was widely accepted. Of course,
wide acceptance is probative of persuasiveness, but not dispositive."[13]
And the reasoning of the opposition was contradictory and unpersua-
sive. It was the near-supermajority in both houses whose reasoning
from the text of the Fourteenth Amendment made textual, and moral,
sense. If such advocates of desegregation had not existed in 1872–75
but only appeared in the 1950s, their better arguments about the facts
should still have carried the day.

CONCLUSION

Our discussion of *Brown* sums things up nicely. Here is what we have
learned. First, we learned that, as a general matter, we must separate
the questions of what the Constitution says and of whether it is legitimate. Most originalists today agree that the nature of language in our
legal system requires an original public meaning method of constitutional interpretation. That is simply the default rule for the interpretation of human communication intended for a public audience, and
particularly of laws intended as public instructions. The question then
becomes whether the original public meaning of the Constitution
creates a just regime worthy of our obedience. Saying that originalism
must somehow justify *Brown* for it to be a legitimate theory of

interpretation gets the question backward. We must first decide what the Constitution says, and only then decide whether what it says is legitimate.

I argued in an earlier chapter that the Constitution the Framers created protected natural rights, created a republican form of government, and was rooted in a legitimate act of popular sovereignty. Even if each of these grounds for legitimacy may be somewhat inadequate, taken together they create a formidable case for constitutional obedience, especially when we take prudential considerations into account. Therefore, I argued, the Constitution as originally understood is just and worthy of our obedience today.

That argument can also justify originalism in another way. It is, of course, possible that modern, nonoriginalist interpretations of the Constitution create a more just regime, more worthy of our obedience. That is surely a debatable proposition. But if you think the original Constitution, in accommodating the competing requirements of legitimate government, successfully created a just regime, then we should be originalists because only *that* interpretation would be consistent with that regime. It may be that other interpretations are more legitimate, but such interpretations would have to be normatively justified and account for deviating from our legal system's approach to "rule of law."

We thus come back to *Brown v. Board*. If the Constitution as originally understood does not require desegregation, perhaps it is not just and worthy of our obedience today. Fortunately, it was only an older flavor of originalism that could not justify *Brown*. That older variety was flawed in its theory, and in any event, no serious originalist abides by that kind of originalism today. Whether it is through a more thorough investigation of the historical materials – which, I have argued, legal thinkers can be adequately equipped to pursue – or through a finer understanding of the distinction between meaning and application (or between sense and reference), originalism can and does justify *Brown v. Board*. The Constitution and its subsequent amendments, as understood by their original public meaning, create a just regime worthy of our continuing obedience today.

8 A CODA ON NONORIGINALISMS

"[T]he provisions of the Constitution are not mathematical
formulas having their essence in their form; they are organic,
living institutions ..."[1]

Justice Oliver Wendell Holmes (1914)

We have now made the positive case for originalism. The reader can
comfortably omit this coda on nonoriginalism and still understand the
case for originalism. But one must surely wonder: Why are so many
people – or at least judges and law professors – nonoriginalist? Why does
a vast majority of the academy and a substantial minority of the general
population object to originalism? What do they offer instead? As
I mentioned before, Justice Scalia famously quipped that originalism
doesn't have to outrun the bear; it just has to run faster than any other
available theory. And it outruns nonoriginalists, who don't have a theory
at all. Nonoriginalists do, however, have a variety of theories. This
chapter briefly explores what they have to offer, and concludes that they
are all unsatisfactory. That will strengthen our case for originalism itself.

As already noted in the Introduction, however, it bears mentioning
that far less separates the best nonoriginalists from the best originalists.
Some advocates of living constitutionalism caricature originalism as per-
mitting only "original expected applications" (for example, originalists
must think the Second Amendment applies only to muskets); as requiring
reliance on narrow and often impossible understandings of the Framers'
specific intent on modern issues of which they could not possibly have
conceived; or as prohibiting flexibility and adaptation. As I have argued
throughout this book, the best argument for originalism recognizes that
the original Constitution can be quite adaptive, and that it is often

capacious in its range of plausible original meanings (but often much less capacious than the living constitutionalist would like it to be).

We begin our assessment of nonoriginalisms by separating out the two questions that form the core of our inquiry. But we take them in reverse order: First, why do nonoriginalists believe we should obey the Constitution (assuming they believe that at all)? That is, what makes the Constitution legitimate? Second, assuming we should obey the Constitution, how should we interpret the Constitution? We take them in reverse order, because if nonoriginalists are to persuade us that we should be free and flexible with the text, they must first and independently justify why the text matters at all.

NONORIGINALIST JUSTIFICATIONS: SETTLEMENT VALUES

We have briefly encountered David Strauss's view on why the text of the Constitution matters. He believes that the Constitution is "legitimate" simply because it is *necessary* to have one – we must settle structural questions one way or another so that we can engage in ordinary politics. It isn't all that important that some questions were settled wrongly – for example, that each state, no matter how small, gets two senators – so long as they were settled. As Strauss writes, the answer to Jefferson's dead-hand-of-the-past problem

> is that our adherence to the written Constitution does not have to depend on veneration of our ancestors or on any acknowledgment of their right to rule us from the grave. The written Constitution is valuable because it provides a common ground among the American people, and in that way makes it possible for us to settle disputes that might otherwise be intractable and destructive. Sometimes, in a familiar formulation, it is more important that things be settled than that they be settled right, and the provisions of the written Constitution settle things. The Constitution tells us the qualifications for various offices, how long a president's term will be, how many senators each state will have, whether there must be jury trials in criminal cases, and many other things. Even if the rules the Constitution prescribes are not the best possible rules, they give us good enough answers to important issues, so

that we do not have to keep reopening those issues all the time. This is an immensely valuable function.[2]

Strauss's view, of course, is that at least most of the questions must have been settled right or with "good enough" answers. After all, his defense of the Constitution would otherwise be a defense of *any* constitution. Ordinary politics occurred in England with a king at the head and an aristocratic House of Lords providing a check against the House of Commons. Although a written constitution creating these institutions would presumably have the same settlement value as ours, I'm not sure Strauss would go along with it. I doubt he would follow a constitution that prohibited trials by jury or that had property qualifications for senators. The question is therefore whether our Constitution is a *good* constitution, and Strauss's answer seems to be that it's good enough for us to follow in some respects, but not all. And therein lies the problem. Who gets to decide which parts to follow and which not to follow, and why? I'm not sure there's a good answer.

Law professor Mark Graber, the author of the Oxford-published *A New Introduction to American Constitutionalism*, makes an argument similar to Strauss, but in more detail. His text is a general introduction to constitutionalism. And yet, he does not devote any treatment to the question of whether our Constitution is just and worthy of our obedience. He devotes much space to making the claim that our Constitution serves many "purposes." By this he does not seem to mean that it serves the purpose of creating a democratic regime or protecting natural rights. Rather, the "purposes" of the Constitution (as he himself admits) are really the purposes of *any* constitution: (1) constitutions "creat[e] a framework" for making and enforcing laws, establish the "rules of [the] game," and serve as precommitments that make ordinary politics possible; (2) they increase legal stability and peaceful cooperation by creating credible commitments; (3) they prevent self-dealing on the part of government officials by restricting some of their power (this might have some normative valence similar to securing liberty and protecting natural rights); (4) they promote the public interest by establishing structures whereby good laws can be passed (here, perhaps, we are no longer talking about *any* constitution); (5) they provide insurance against an uncertain future; (6) they enshrine national aspirations; and (7) and they serve as a tool of compromise to allow ordinary politics to operate.[3]

It would appear that most of these constitutional purposes could be served by undemocratic constitutions, even by constitutions that don't secure the blessings of liberty. Even the North Korean constitution, for example, establishes the rules of the game. Any constitution, even the most illiberal one, can similarly create legal stability. A regime can be very stable and yet be a very bad one. A one-party dictatorship can establish rules to prevent self-dealing among party officials (though the head official is usually exempt). All constitutions that are at least somewhat enduring provide insurance against an uncertain future, enshrine national aspirations (for brotherhood, solidarity, or a proletariat perhaps), and allow ruling elites to compromise among each other.

Of course, that's not to say that our constitution isn't good and necessary partly because it also sets our rules of the game, or because it also promotes stability; it's only to say that this doesn't justify obedience to our *particular* constitution. If we had a less democratic and liberal constitution, it would seem that it would still serve many of the same purposes described by Graber and Strauss and would thus be justified in commanding our obedience. Of course, Graber and Strauss do not really believe that. As already explained, they believe quite explicitly that the constitution also has to be a *good* one – it has to get at mostly right answers most of the time. For example, Graber discusses separation of powers, representation, and federalism as creating the conditions for the passing of good laws. I agree. But the question then remains: If we owe our Constitution obedience because it settles most questions mostly right, when and why are we allowed to deviate from the Constitution's commands? As before, I am not sure there is a good answer.

We now turn to how nonoriginalists think we should *interpret* the Constitution. That is because even if nonoriginalists do not provide persuasive reasons for constitutional obedience, they still claim the text matters at least some of the time. If they claimed the Constitution's text mattered not at all, I suspect they would not be taken very seriously. So the question becomes: How do they suggest we interpret the text?

NONORIGINALIST CONTENDER I: THE COMMON LAW CONSTITUTION

Perhaps the most potent opponent of originalism is a version of living constitutionalism more helpfully described as common law constitutionalism. The idea is that the Constitution evolves in much the same way as the common law has evolved over many centuries. To understand this theory we must know something about the history of the common law.

The United States is a common law country, where all jurisdictions except Louisiana (which had been a French territory) are common law jurisdictions. We inherited the common law from England, in which the common law developed for many centuries as a rival system of lawmaking to the "civil law" system of Continental Europe. The civil law system derives from Roman law, and is very straightforward. All legal obligations flow directly from statutes and detailed legal codes. For much of history these legal codes were formulated by royal monarchs, though today the codes can be enacted by popular assemblies.

The common law is different. It is a system where judges discern the law on a case-by-case basis by looking to the accumulated wisdom of previous precedents to see whether there is an applicable legal rule or principle. Judges look at the cases before them and decide whether there is a precedent on point. Have other common law judges addressed this particular situation in the past? What was the rule laid down in those cases? Can that rule apply in this case, too? If there is a difference of relevance in the present case, the judges decide whether the rule in prior cases has to be extended or modified. Perhaps an altogether new rule is appropriate for the new circumstance. Judges will make such decisions on the basis of their best understanding of what prior decisions require, but also on considerations of public policy and social welfare. In the past, judges would consider "reason" and "natural law" in creating new rules.

One can immediately see several advantages to this system of lawmaking. It is not freewheeling. It does not give judges unlimited discretion. Judges quite properly look to precedent. The advantage of the common law is that precedents bind in like cases – so the rule of law is established – but it allows for flexibility when cases have important

differences. Compare that to the abstract and detailed legal codes of
the civil law, in which there is little flexibility.

Much of our law today still derives from this common law method
of judging. Contract law, property law, and tort law are all still rooted
in the common law. But the common law operates within a much
broader legal framework. State legislatures (not to mention Congress)
often enact statutes in these traditional common law areas. Tort law
used to handle the development of drugs and the liability of pharma-
cists, drug companies, and so on, until the Federal Food, Drug, and
Cosmetic Act "preempted" much of the field. Do common law courts
ignore federal law and regulations in this area? No. The democratically
enacted laws take precedence. That means that if the enacted laws
override old common law rules, the enacted laws prevail.

That's not all that different from how things were in England.
Although some common law judges at important constitutional moments
claimed that their power was above both the king *and* Parliament, for
much of common law history, judges operated in what we might call
the *interstices* of enacted statute law. That is, as Parliament became
more active in passing laws in the 1300s–1700s, common law judges
only filled in the gaps where Parliament's laws did not direct the
outcome (and where old precedents did not dictate a particular outcome). Thus, even in England, if Parliament legislated, it was typically
considered supreme.[4]

This system connects to living constitutionalism. David Strauss is
the foremost proponent of the idea that the Constitution ought to be
interpreted through the common law method. To a large extent, the
Constitution has been interpreted through that method: the Supreme
Court constantly looks to precedent to decide how a particular case
should come out. Often the text of the Constitution gets little more than
a cursory (or courtesy) review. Whether an action violates the First
Amendment will have very little to do with the words "Congress shall
make no law . . . abridging the freedom of speech" and much more to do
with whether it is a content-based restriction, whether it gets "strict" or
"intermediate" scrutiny, and so on – concepts that have developed over
time in various precedents.

Strauss offers four reasons why common law constitutionalism is
superior to originalism.[5] First, he argues that originalism requires that
lawyers do history, but that lawyers are not historians and there is no

reason to think they'll be particularly good at doing history. On the other hand, "The common law approach requires judges and lawyers to be, well, judges and lawyers. Reasoning from precedent, with occasional resort to basic notions of fairness and good policy, is what judges and lawyers do."

We took up this criticism in an earlier chapter. Consider a few additional points. What if the only available precedent is one hundred years old? Or even just twenty years old? Understanding precedent sometimes requires understanding the background of the case – the background concepts and facts that may be somewhat unfamiliar to modern eyes and ears. That also requires doing history. More still, how do lawyers determine good policy? Presumably they look at the history of certain social practices and policies and decide on the basis of those whether some policy will be good or bad. Social policy does not exist in a vacuum. It exists in a social and historical context, and so requires judges to do history, too.

Strauss's second point in defense of common law constitutionalism is that it is more justifiable because it draws on accumulated wisdom, whereas originalism, he argues, focuses only on the time of enactment and ignores subsequent practices. It is unsatisfactory to focus only on the time of enactment, he writes, because "[i]t is one thing to be commanded by a legislature we elected last year" but "quite another to be commanded by the people who assembled in the Constitutional Convention and the state ratifying conventions in the late eighteenth century." Yet this statement turns everything on its head. It is the *living constitutionalist* who thinks decisions made by judges – even if those decisions are the culmination of various precedents – is the final word on the Constitution, compared to what last year's Congress might have said. In other words, the original understanding of the text might allow Congress to do x, Congress seeks to do x, but it is the living constitutionalist judges who can still say we think the Constitution no longer permits Congress to do x. It is the living constitutionalist who says, "This unoriginalist precedent from the 1950s trumps what Congress in 2017 wants to do, even though Congress's reading of the Constitution is more plausible as a matter of the text's original meaning." To David Strauss, the 1950s, unoriginalist, undemocratic precedent can trump what yesterday's democratic, perhaps originalist Congress wants to do.

But moreover, who's to say that courts have a monopoly on accumulated wisdom? I think Congress can also learn from what past Congresses have done. Congress routinely passes laws that build on existing laws, or that amend, adjust, or extend them. Congress and the state legislatures also have an entire history of accumulated wisdom they can look to. It makes more sense to permit the Constitution's original meaning to circumscribe the limits of what democratic majorities can do, but otherwise leave these democratic majorities to rely on their own accumulated wisdom to decide on the best public policies.

Strauss's third point is that common law constitutionalism is what we actually do. And in elaboration, he contends that America without this method would "look" very different than the country we have today. He posits an America in which states *can* segregate schools, in which the federal government *can* discriminate against women, and so on. But that misses the larger point. Just because the Constitution does not *require* something – say, gender equality – doesn't mean we won't do it as a matter of public policy. The abortion laws in all fifty states were well on the way to being dramatically liberalized before *Roe v. Wade* constitutionalized the issue and crystallized a perpetual opposition – perhaps to the detriment of the pro-choice position. Gay marriage was well on its way to being enacted in several if not dozens of states before *Obergefell v. Hodges*. So when Strauss says that an originalist Constitution would create a universe in which Congress "can" do bad things, one must remember that the real question is whether Congress is *required* to do something bad. Our Constitution does not, cannot, and was never intended to enshrine in fundamental law all that is good and just in the world. That Congress "can" still do some bad things if it wanted to does not seem a very strong argument against originalism.

Strauss's fourth and final argument in defense of the common law approach is that it is more candid. In a sense, he's right. It is certainly more candid to admit, as Strauss does, that under his approach judges make freewheeling policy choices. But that sidesteps the larger question. Is our Constitution as originally interpreted and are our ordinary democratic institutions *amenable* to the common law method? To some extent, sure. As we have seen, the text cannot possibly answer every question. There will be hard cases that will require the various branches of government and the people themselves to debate issues of constitutional meaning. But it hardly stands to reason that because some judges will sometimes have to make freewheeling policy choices, they always should do so. Where possible, in a society like ours, the people and their representatives should make such choices. The problem with Strauss's common law constitutionalism is that it is unclear why judges should be permitted to make freewheeling policy choices contrary to the policy choices of our representatives, when the latter are acting consistently with the restrictions we the people enacted upon them in the Constitution.

NONORIGINALIST CONTENDER II: A MORAL THEORY OF ENHANCING DEMOCRACY

There are two other plausible contenders to originalism, propounded by two of the greatest legal thinkers of the late twentieth century, Ronald Dworkin and John Hart Ely. It may seem odd to group these two together: Dworkin is famous for a "moral reading" of the Constitution, for advancing an interpretation that makes the Constitution the best it can be; Ely, on the other hand, ostensibly eschewed any moral reading of the Constitution whatsoever in favor of a process-oriented view. But I think we can productively lump them together because the same impetus drove both Dworkin and Ely to choose their respective interpretive approaches: enhancing the democratic legitimacy of the Constitution.

Dworkin believed in interpreting the Constitution so that it is the best it can be. Dworkin claimed that a progressive, moral reading of the Constitution in fact *improved* democracy even where it appeared to flout the popular will. He stated his position in various ways. Most succinctly: "Democracy means government subject to conditions – we might call these the 'democratic' conditions – of equal status for all citizens."[6] These conditions are necessary because otherwise the democratic decisions of a majority would have no binding force on those who disagree with the political decisions of the majority.

Thus, to be legitimate, a constitutional democracy requires that each citizen have a *part* in the collective decisions, a *stake* in those decisions, and *independence* from them. The first condition supports constitutional decisions requiring universal suffrage, effective elections, and perhaps equal representation, as well as nearly total free speech rights; only that way can the citizens have full participation in democratic decision-making. The second condition requires political decisions to treat every person with "equal concern," and the third condition requires that the political community not dictate what a citizen thinks about matters of political, moral, or ethical judgment.[7]

Dworkin justified the antidemocratic decisions of the Supreme Court by changing the inquiry to one in which we ask if democracy *properly understood* is *enhanced*. Thus, if a popular majority passes a law banning flag burning, the Court is more democratic, or at least democratic in a *better* sense, by striking down the ban:

> If the court's decision is correct – if laws against flag-burning do in fact violate the democratic conditions set out in the Constitution as these have been interpreted and formed by American history – the decision is not anti-democratic, but, on the contrary, improves democracy.... No one's power to participate in a self-governing community has been worsened, ... [n]o one's equality has been compromised, ... [n]o one has been cheated of the ethical advantages of a role in principled deliberation.... If the court had not intervened ... everyone would have been worse off, in all the dimensions of democracy, and it would be perverse to regard that as in any way or sense a democratic victory.[8]

Dworkin, like Strauss, thus claimed that the moral reading of the Constitution is how judges *in fact* interpret the Constitution. This is the "fit" part of Dworkin's theory – his "moral reading" "fits" the constitutional history and precedents. Dworkin's theory is not exclusive of Strauss's theory; it may be that the Constitution has evolved in a common law manner over time as judges employed their particular moral readings of the constitutional text.

Is the moral reading persuasive? Certainly its "fit" component is somewhat persuasive. It explains many constitutional precedents on the basis of an overarching moral theory that seeks to enhance democracy. Nevertheless, it is not a new criticism to suggest that Dworkin's constitutional views also happily supported his political precommitments. It was often said that Dworkin's theory always had "happy endings."[9] Decisions that he liked (prohibiting flag burning, constitutionalizing a right to an abortion) were often consistent with his theory, and those he did not were often inconsistent with his theory. Dworkin himself acknowledged this criticism, though I do not think he ever provided a persuasive counterexample.[10]

More fundamentally, any moral reading of the Constitution demands an answer to two questions: (1) Which moral reading is better than others? (And what if people disagree?) and (2) Who gets to decide? What if the Congress and the president each have a different moral reading of the Constitution, and enact laws or take actions accordingly, but the unelected Justices of the Supreme Court operate with a different moral reading? Why should the Supreme Court's version prevail?

The first question is more fundamental: Which moral reading ought we to adopt? If you believe that the role of text in our linguistic and legal systems does not require originalism, then there is no self-evident reason why Dworkin's reading is wrong. His moral reading strikes some balance between liberty and self-government, much as the Founders' understanding did; his conception of liberty and self-government is simply a different one. If we should be originalists because the original Constitution is just, then maybe we should be Dworkinians because Dworkin's moral reading is *more* just.

It may be just a matter of deciding which is more persuasive. It just so happens that Dworkin's moral reading is often consistent with progressivism. He does not believe that contract and property rights are fundamental to freedom, for example.[11] Originalism is *more often* consistent with conservatism or libertarianism, although honest conservatives and libertarians will recognize that there are parts of the Constitution with which they disagree. While originalism might sometimes be a rationalization for political decisions, originalism at least ostensibly provides a standard that is morally neutral from a contemporary perspective.

None of this will matter, of course, to an originalist who thinks that the theory of language in our legal system requires us to be originalist. Perhaps a better defense of originalism thus begins with that proposition: that our understanding of the rule of law and the values it serves requires us to interpret *any* law with its original public meaning. Whether the Constitution, so interpreted, is a "moral" constitution demanding our continued obedience is a separate inquiry altogether.

NONORIGINALIST CONTENDER III: A PROCESS
THEORY OF ENHANCING DEMOCRACY

John Hart Ely, in his famous *Democracy and Distrust* written in 1980,
similarly presented a theory of interpretation that purports to enhance
democracy. In his case it is often described as a "representation-
reinforcing" interpretation. Ely rejected the possibility of discovering
fundamental values to supplement the open-ended texture of the
Constitution's clauses.[12] Nevertheless, the text is still open-ended:
something has to supplement it. Ely argued that the Court could interpret these provisions to provide better *process* for democratic decision-
making; this could include "clearing the channels of political change
on the one hand, and ... correcting certain kinds of discrimination
against minorities on the other," as the Warren Court had done.[13]
Such a "representation-reinforcing approach to judicial review, unlike
its rival value-protecting approach, is not inconsistent with, but on the
contrary (and quite by design) entirely supportive of, the underlying
premises of the American system of representative democracy."[14]

The problem is that although Ely recognized that the constitutional
text needs supplementation, and recognized the impossibility of discovering external substantive values to provide that supplementation,
he maintained that his process-oriented view was itself not a value
judgment. It seems to me that Ely was not really so different from
those scholars (like Dworkin) whom he disavowed for seeking to
vindicate substantive values. By choosing to emphasize representation
and process, he ignored the very real possibility that the Constitution
did mean to protect *some* kind of substantive rights as well. Indeed, we
have seen that the Founders expected the Constitution not only to
enable representative government but also to protect certain rights.
Ely's prioritizing of the process-oriented purposes over these rights
purposes was itself a value choice.

An example may illustrate. Ely acknowledged that our Constitution
"has always been substantially concerned with preserving liberty."[15]
But he nevertheless suggested that the Supreme Court's having read
out of the Constitution the right to bear arms (remember, he was
writing in 1980) and the freedom to contract indicated that Americans
expected the Constitution to protect *process* more than substantive

rights. But this is to reject the choices of the Framers and replace them with the choices of subsequent generations. It is not at all obvious that Ely's value judgment was superior to the value judgments made by the Framers.

The same caution made about Dworkin must now be made about Ely. If you think that originalism is required by the very nature of a language in our legal system, then none of this much matters. We have to be originalists whether or not the Constitution sufficiently establishes or "reinforces" representation. If the Constitution does not sufficiently do so, that may be a reason for amending the Constitution or abandoning it altogether. But it is not an argument against originalism. On the other hand, to those who believe any interpretation is only as good as the results that interpretation ultimately creates, I would still maintain that the balance of values maintained by the original Constitution is superior to an interpretive method that values only process and not rights.

TEXTUALISM

Finally, some argue that "textualism" is an alternative to originalism. I once attended a conference with hundreds of lawyers and academics on the topic of textualism and originalism. Almost everyone seemed to think there was a difference between the two. Textualists just look at the words; originalists look at historical practice, original intentions, and so on. Many scholars, both liberal and conservative, insisted almost defensively, "I'm a textualist, not an originalist!"

I'm not quite sure what that means. Isn't textualism just understanding what words *mean*? And don't words have meaning only in the context in which they are used? Go back to bloodletting in the streets. Devoid of any context whatsoever, the doctor would be prosecuted for drawing the blood of his patient. But what about within the social and historical context? Surely no bloodletting in the streets *means* there shall be no fighting in the streets. Surely it does not *mean* that doctors can't be good Samaritans. Even if we suppose that the text "means" the doctor can't treat the patient, our legal system may also have an existing rule that provides an exception for emergency situations.

In that case, there wouldn't be any difference between textualism and originalism on either the question of meaning or the question of what legal effect that meaning has.

Two constitutional examples can illustrate the point. Some used to suggest that there is a difference between a textualist interpretation and an originalist interpretation of the First Amendment. Justice Hugo Black famously said of its injunction, "Congress shall make no law . . . abridging the freedom of speech," that "no law" means "no law."[16] He was what we might call a First Amendment absolutist. Others would point out, however, that the founding generation had all sorts of laws infringing free speech – laws against incitement, fighting words, and so on. Does that mean an "originalist" interpretation, which looks at this history and social context, diverges from the text of the First Amendment? I don't see how that's the case. Surely the history and social context help inform us what the meaning of the words "the freedom of speech" is; that is, perhaps this "freedom" was never thought to include incitement to violence. Or perhaps the historical practice informs us what "abridging" means. Alternatively, the pre-existing rules against incitement or libel may cabin what would otherwise be the full effect of the literal meaning of the First Amendment's words. In either case, originalist methods help us understand what the text actually means, or what legal effect it actually has.

The other example is a bit more complex but still of general interest. A hugely controversial topic in the legal academy is sovereign immunity, the legal notion that a state cannot be sued in court without its consent. Did the state not pay you proper wages? Did its officers commit a tort against you? Too bad – the state doesn't have to consent to let you sue it to recover your proper wages or any damages. You might just be out of luck. The idea is that the "sovereign" – here the state or the federal government – is "immune" from liability unless it agrees to be sued.

Well, can the *federal* government force a *state* to be sued? That is, can the federal government pass a law pursuant to its commerce power that establishes, say, fair labor standards, but that also declares that a state employee aggrieved by the state's failure to abide by these standards can sue the state in federal court without the state's consent? Put differently, can the federal government *abrogate* or *eliminate* a state's sovereign immunity?

I'm simplifying a bit, but most textualists, both liberal and conservative, will say yes. They'll say that the Constitution says nothing about sovereign immunity, and so why can't the federal government pass a law pursuant to its enumerated powers that also allows private citizens to sue the states to enforce it? There's nothing in the text that stops them from doing it. Originalists, on the other hand, will say that sovereign immunity is a "background principle of law" and that we aren't guided *just* by the text. We assume that when the Constitution was enacted, this background principle was presumed to be intact.

Is this an example of a true difference between textualism and originalism? I don't think so. I think the history of sovereign immunity as a background principle of law actually informs what the text means. Can you force a state to be sued in federal court? Well, Article III of the Constitution grants the federal judiciary power over "cases" or "controversies." As Caleb Nelson has shown, if the state never agreed to be sued by a private individual, then there simply wouldn't be a *case or controversy.*[17] So the text accounts for this originalist history within the words "case" or "controversy." Unless a state consented to be sued, no "case" or "controversy" would form and there could be no federal judicial power over the case. Even if the background principle of sovereign immunity cannot be baked into the meaning of "case" or "controversy," it still might be a preexisting legal rule that the text of the Constitution just left alone.[18] In either case, originalism and textualism still amount to the same thing.

My general point is that if originalism means looking at the text, the historical background, the historical purposes, the intent of the authors, linguistic conventions, and so on to try to assess what the words of the Constitution (or any legal text) *mean*, and subsequently what legal effect that meaning has, then that seems no different than textualism.

For whatever reason I seem to be a minority voice on this question. Either way, thinking in these terms helps clarify what most people mean by originalism. It is precisely as I just described: originalists look to several clues to understand what the constitutional text means. They look to linguistic and grammatical conventions. They look to the purposes for which the words were deployed. Perhaps they even look to the specific intent of the more prominent founders. We primarily look to the words themselves, but that is not enough, because words have meaning only in context.

There is one variant of textualism that merits separate treatment. David Strauss suggests that it may be legitimate to interpret the Constitution with a *contemporary* textual meaning.[19] He uses the example of the Sixth Amendment right for an accused "to have the assistance of counsel for his defence." There is no doubt that the founding generation would not have understood this to mean the government must pay for the accused's lawyer if he can't afford one. Just over fifty years ago, however, the Supreme Court said that the Constitution does require that.

That is not an originalist interpretation. But might it be textualist? It just so happens that this interpretation is consistent with a plausible modern reading of the text. If the accused has the right "to have the assistance of counsel," isn't it perfectly plausible to think that it means he has the right to a lawyer even if he cannot afford one? The Supreme Court could have chosen a number of interpretations, and it just so happens that the one it chose is consistent with a plausible modern reading of the text.

That's not a crazy theory. It seems to me it still suffers from the same problems as before. First, it turns out that most living constitutionalist interpretations are *not* consistent with a modern reading of the text, and yet these nonoriginalists somehow still justify them. Perhaps Strauss's theory here can be legitimate insofar as it affects only those doctrines truly tied to a plausible modern reading of the text. I don't think there are many. But as we've mentioned before, the biggest criticism is that this method of interpretation implies that our law is determined by *accidental* changes in language over time. No authoritative source of law – not the Framers, not the Ratifiers, not the people themselves in subsequent acts of amendment – decided that the law should change. The law merely happened to change based on accidental drifts in language. Who enacted such accidental drifts into the law? You see the problem. As far as I am aware, no theory of politics or government would justify the use of "semantic drift" as a rule of legal change.

To conclude, none of these nonoriginalist theories outruns Justice Scalia's bear. It may be that Dworkin's interpretation or Ely's interpretation creates a more just Constitution. But each chooses certain values at the expense of others. The Founders, as we learned, embraced competing values – republican government that checked the excesses of democracy, the protection of rights, popular sovereignty – and did their best to accommodate them in the Constitution's text. Whether Dworkin's or Ely's Constitution is more just than the Founders' Constitution is something the reader will have to decide.

But irrespective of whether these nonoriginalist theories create a more legitimate constitution, they nevertheless approach the inquiry backward. They first justify why we should obey the Constitution at all, no matter how we interpret its words, and only then decide what is the best way to interpret those words to achieve their preferred values. Most originalists today approach these questions from the other direction. They accept that the original public understanding *is* what the text – what any public text intended as an instruction – means. Only then do they ask whether the Constitution is a good constitution.

EPILOGUE

On December 7, 1787, the townsmen of Richmond, Berkshire County, Massachusetts, convened "to consider of, and examine the Federal Constitution." They met no fewer than four times. On their third meeting, they elected a delegate to send to the state convention that would convene on the second Wednesday in January 1788, for the purpose of "assenting to and ratifying" – or rejecting – the proposed Constitution. They met one more time to decide whether and how to instruct their delegate. They voted "That the Town think not proper to adopt the Constitution as it now stands."[1]

This scene – individuals of a town, sometimes only forty or fifty people, gathering to debate the Constitution and decide how their representatives in the state convention would vote – repeated across the entire state. And even towns not officially entitled to representatives at the convention – because they were too small for representation in the lower house of the state legislatures – met, deliberated, and sent delegates. The townsmen of Dalton, also in Berkshire County, declared that because "forming themselves into Society and establishing a frame of Government is the common & equal Right of all Men," so long as they had a "Competency of Understanding and common Sense," they too should have a "Voice" in the business of ratification.

Although the towns of Massachusetts were unique in their mode of deliberations, the intensity of their debates and their degree of public participation were replicated across the United States. The people of America understood, as Alexander Hamilton had written, "that it seems to have been reserved to the people of this country, by their conduct and example, to decide the important question, whether

134

societies of men are really capable or not of establishing good government from reflection and choice, or whether they are forever destined
to depend for their political constitutions on accident and force."[2]

For its time, the ratification of the Constitution was an extraordin-
arily democratic act. Perhaps no time before or since has a people so
thoroughly understood that their choice of government would set the
course for, and determine the safety, liberty, and happiness of, millions
of men and women then living and yet unborn. Perhaps no time before
or since has so great a proportion of the people of a country understood the question before them, digested with meticulous detail the
provisions of the constitution they would judge, and comprehended
with such solemnity the theories behind, and likely consequences of,
what they were enacting.

The people of this country banded together in an extraordinary
moment of Founding. Can one imagine this exercise being repeated
today? It is, of course, possible that we could create a document as
short and concise, as technical and yet uplifting, as the Constitution of
1787. But it is not probable. One need only look across the pond to
the European Union's recent abortive attempt to frame a constitution.
At nearly 450 clauses and an additional 200 pages of protocols,[3] can
one imagine the citizens of Massachusetts – or the citizens of any
country – exercising the kind of democratic deliberation that occurred
in this country in its Founding moment?

The Founding generation gave us an improvement in government –
an improvement in a way of life – unlikely to be surpassed by any
contemporary generation. They gave us a government, conceived in
liberty and dedicated to the proposition that all men are created equal,
that has endured for more than two centuries and has to a large
measure redeemed its founding promises. They have formed a debt
against the living today. We owe it to them – nay, we owe it to
ourselves – to discharge this debt by a proportionate obedience to what
they have done.

NOTES

INTRODUCTION

1 Letter from Thomas Jefferson to James Madison (Sept. 6, 1789), *in* THE ESSENTIAL JEFFERSON 176, 176, 179 (Jean M. Yarbrough ed., 2006) (emphasis in original).

2 David A. Strauss, *Common Law, Common Ground, and Jefferson's Principle*, 112 YALE L.J. 1717, 1717 (2003).

3 DAVID A. STRAUSS, THE LIVING CONSTITUTION 44 (2010).

4 Paul A. Brest, *The Misconceived Quest for the Original Understanding*, 60 B.U. L. REV. 204, 225 (1980).

5 *See, e.g.,* RANDY E. BARNETT, RESTORING THE LOST CONSTITUTION: THE PRESUMPTION OF LIBERTY 14–25 (2004).

6 Seth Ackerman, *Burn the Constitution*, 2 JACOBIN, Mar. 26, 2011, https://www.jacobinmag.com/2011/03/burn-the-constitution.

7 Louis Michael Seidman, Opinion, *Let's Give Up on the Constitution*, N.Y. TIMES (Dec. 30, 2012), http://www.nytimes.com/2012/12/31/opinion/lets-give-up-on-the-constitution.html.

8 SANFORD LEVINSON, OUR UNDEMOCRATIC CONSTITUTION 9, 11–12 (2006).

9 Letter from James Madison to Thomas Jefferson (Feb. 4, 1790), *in* THE MIND OF THE FOUNDER: SOURCES OF THE POLITICAL THOUGHT OF JAMES MADISON 176, 177 (Marvin Meyers ed., rev. ed. 1981) (emphasis in original). The quoted language differs from what Madison originally wrote Jefferson. In the original letter, Madison stated that the improvements made by the dead form a "charge" against the living. Letter from James Madison to Thomas Jefferson (Feb. 4, 1790), *in* 13 THE PAPERS OF JAMES MADISON, January 20, 1790–March 31, 1791, 18–21 (Charles Hobson et al., ed., 1981). The letter Madison revised late in life includes the word "debt," as well as other cosmetic changes that improve the paragraph's cadence. The National Archives explains the timing of Madison's revisions. *Madison on "The Earth Belongs to the Living": Editorial Note*, FOUNDERS ONLINE, https://founders.archives.gov/documents/Jefferson/01-16-02-0081 (last visited Mar. 7, 2017).

1 THE ORIGINS OF ORIGINALISM

1 Edwin Meese III, Attorney Gen., Dep't of Justice, Speech Before the American Bar Association (July 9, 1985), *in* ORIGINALISM: A QUARTER-CENTURY OF DEBATE 47, 53 (Steven G. Calabresi ed., 2007).

2 Miranda v. Arizona, 384 U.S. 436 (1966).

3 Mapp v. Ohio, 367 U.S. 643 (1961). The Court had already required the exclusionary rule in federal cases for some decades. *See* Weeks v. United States, 232 U.S. 383 (1914).

4 *See* Michael Stokes Paulsen, *Dirty Harry and the Real Constitution*, 64 U. CHI. L. REV. 1457, 1484–91 (1997) (book review).

5 Edwin Meese III, Attorney Gen., Dep't of Justice, Speech Before the American Bar Association (July 9, 1985), *supra* note 1; *see also* Speech by Attorney General Edwin Meese III Before the American Bar Association on July 9, 1985, FEDER-ALIST SOC´Y, http://www.fed-soc.org/publications/detail/the-great-debate-attorney-general-ed-meese-iii-july-9-1985 (last visited Mar. 4, 2017).

6 Robert H. Bork, *Neutral Principles and Some First Amendment Problems*, 47 IND. L.J. 1, 1 (1971).

7 *Id.* at 17.

8 *See* Justice William J. Brennan, Speech to the Text and Teaching Symposium, Georgetown University (Oct. 12, 1985), *in* ORIGINALISM: A QUARTER-CENTURY OF DEBATE, *supra* note 1, at 55, 61. The text is also conveniently available at Speech by Justice William J. Brennan, Jr. at Georgetown University on Oct. 12, 1985, FEDERALIST SOC´Y, http://www.fed-soc.org/publica tions/detail/the-great-debate-justice-william-j-brennan-jr-october-12–1985. (last visited Mar. 4, 2017).

9 For an interesting originalist account of the Eighth Amendment suggesting that under some circumstances the death penalty might become unconstitutional, see John F. Stinneford, *The Original Meaning of "Unusual": The Eighth Amendment as a Bar to Cruel Innovation*, 102 NW. U. L. REV. 1739, 1821–22 (2008).

10 Paul A. Brest, *The Misconceived Quest for the Original Understanding*, 60 B.U. L. REV. 204 (1980).

11 H. Jefferson Powell, *The Original Understanding of Original Intent*, 98 HARV. L. REV. 885 (1985).

12 Omychund v. Barker, 26 Eng. Rep. 15, 23 (Ch. 1744) (Mansfield, L.J.) ("[A] statute very seldom can take in all cases, therefore the common law, *that works itself pure* by rules drawn from the fountain of justice, is for this reason superior to an act of parliament."). According to Frederick Schauer, Lon Fuller made this phrase famous. *See* FREDERICK SCHAUER, THINKING LIKE A LAWYER 105 (2009); LON L. FULLER, THE LAW IN QUEST OF ITSELF 140 (1940) ("[T]he common law works itself pure and adapts itself to the needs of a new day.").

13 For this theory, *see, e.g.*, Gary Lawson & Guy Seidman, *Originalism as a Legal Enterprise*, 23 CONST. COMMENT. 47 (2006). For a discussion of the implications of the political ignorance of the ratifying public for originalism, *see* Ilya Somin, *Originalism and Political Ignorance*, 97 MINN. L. REV. 625 (2012).

14 For examples of law professors taking Powell's argument to mean as much, *see* Caleb Nelson, *Originalism and Interpretive Conventions*, 70 U. CHI. L. REV 519, 524–25 & nn. 19–21 (2003).

15 For one of the prominent exceptions, *see* Larry Alexander, *Originalism, The Why and the What*, 82 FORDHAM L. REV. 539 (2013).

16 For a retort to the arguments against using the various notes from the Constitutional Convention, *see* Vasan Kesavan & Michael Stokes Paulsen, *The Interpretive Force of the Constitution's Secret Drafting History*, 91 GEO. L.J. 1113 (2003).

17 1 WILLIAM BLACKSTONE, COMMENTARIES ON THE LAWS OF ENGLAND *60–61.

18 For an introduction to the concept of the "funnel of abstraction" in statutory interpretation, see WILLIAM N. ESKRIDGE, JR. ET AL., CASES AND MATERIALS ON STATUTORY INTERPRETATION 297–99 (2012).

19 William Baude and Stephen Sachs have written on this question of legal meaning versus legal effect in a recent and important law review article. William Baude & Stephen E. Sachs, *The Law of Interpretation*, 130 HARV. L. REV. 1079 (2017).

20 *See* Randy Barnett, *The Original Meaning of the Commerce Clause*, 68 U. CHI. L. REV. 101 (2001).

21 A good place to review some of the original understanding of the Commerce Clause is David Currie's work on constitutional interpretation in the early Congresses, which routinely enacted statutes to improve navigation and otherwise facilitate commerce. *See, e.g.*, DAVID P. CURRIE, THE CONSTITUTION IN CONGRESS: THE FEDERALIST PERIOD, 1789–1801, at 57, 70–72 (1997); DAVID P. CURRIE, THE CONSTITUTION IN CONGRESS: THE JEFFERSONIANS, 1801–1829, at 99, n. 88, 275, 288 (2001); DAVID P. CURRIE, THE CONSTITUTION IN CONGRESS: DEMOCRATS AND WHIGS, 1829–1861, at 13–15 (2005). Currie summarized in his second volume: "Since 1790 Congress had consistently and without objection acted on the understanding that it was competent to facilitate as well as to regulate commerce." THE JEFFERSONIANS, *supra*, at 275.

22 For competing views on the original meaning of the Fourteenth Amendment's Privileges or Immunities Clause, see Kurt T. Lash, *The Fourteenth Amendment and the Privileges and Immunities of American Citizenship* (2014) (arguing it was intended to incorporate the bill of rights against the states); John C. Eastman, *Re-evaluating the Privileges or Immunities Clause*, 6 CHAP. L. REV. 123 (2003) (arguing it protects economic liberties); Philip Hamburger, *Privileges or*

Immunities, 105 NW. U. L. REV. 61 (2015) (arguing it was intended merely to apply the "Comity Clause" rights of Article IV of the original Constitution to blacks).

23　Although I do not discuss theories of precedent in any detail in this book, the interested reader should consult Randy J. Kozel, *Originalism and the Precedent Fallback*, 68 VAND L. REV. 105 (2015); Gary Lawson, *The Constitutional Case against Precedent*, 17 HARV. J.L. & PUB. POLY 23 (1994); Gary Lawson, *Mostly Unconstitutional: The Case against Precedent Revisited*, 5 AVE MARIA L. REV. 1 (2007) (revising and extending his arguments); John McGinnis & Michael Rappaport, *Reconciling Originalism and Precedent*, 103 NW. U. L. REV. 803 (2009).

2　THE MEANING OF MEANING

1　Gary Lawson, *On Reading Recipes . . . and Constitutions*, 85 GEO. L.J. 1823, 1834 (1997).

2　My discussion of Barnett and writtenness is drawn from RANDY E. BARNETT, RESTORING THE LOST CONSTITUTION: THE PRESUMPTION OF LIBERTY 100–09 (2004).

3　KEITH E. WHITTINGTOn, CONSTITUTIONAL INTERPRETATION: TEXTUAL MEANING, ORIGINAL INTENT, AND JUDICIAL REVIEW 50 (1999).

4　DAVID A. STRAUSS, THE LIVING CONSTITUTION 107 (2010).

5　For an account of such "secondary rules of change" as compared to a system's primary rules of conduct, see H. L. A. HART, THE CONCEPT OF LAW 79–99 (3d. ed. 2012).

6　As this book goes to press, no scholar of which I am aware has made the argument that the form of a constitution, i.e., its writtenness or unwrittenness, plays a role in its "secondary" rules of change (and recognition) but not in its existing "primary" rules that govern our current behavior. I defend this thesis in more detail in a forthcoming work.

7　BARNETT, *supra* note 2, at 103.

8　WHITTINGTON, *supra* note 3, at 59.

9　JACK BALKIN, LIVING ORIGINALISM 35–36 (2011).

10　*Id.*

11　Lawrence B. Solum, District of Columbia v. Heller *and Originalism*, 103 NW. U. L. REV. 923, 945 (2009).

12　*Id.* at 946.

13　Lawson, *supra* note 1.

14　Andrew B. Coan, *The Irrelevance of Writtenness in Constitutional Interpretation*, 158 U. PA. L. REV. 1025, 1049 (2010).

15　KENT GREENAWALT, INTERPRETING THE CONSTITUTION 20 (2015).

16 For example, Greenawalt offers a parallel to a private instruction from a mother to a guardian that her son should become a "skilled craftsman, such as a carpenter or tailor, or a clerk." *Id.* at 22. It transpires that her son has great aptitude for law, and Greenawalt suggests that the guardian "might claim a kind of implied exception for decisions that he deems to be gravely wrong." *Id.* at 27. The implication is, as Greenawalt notes later, that perhaps "original understanding . . . even if perceivable, should not be conclusive." *Id.* at 41. But I'm not sure that proves that in clear cases of contradiction original understanding should not be conclusive. First, I would suggest that it's rather clear that the initial instruction from the mother to the guardian was an exceedingly poor one, in that it did not allow for adaptation to future circumstances that easily should have been anticipated. If that was the case with our constitution, then surely it should have been abandoned at an early stage for something much more adaptive and capacious. Second, to the extent this issue bears on how a nonoriginalist would interpret the Constitution, it goes to show that nonoriginalists would merely replace the meaning of the Constitution with whatever they think it *should* say, according to their own particular lights. After all, it could very well be that the boy's mother was in fact more perceptive than the guardian – perhaps all lawyers are irredeemably corrupt!

17 For more on the distinction between legal meaning and effect, I refer the reader again to William Baude & Stephen E. Sachs, *The Law of Interpretation,* 130 HARV. L. REV. 1079 (2017).

18 William Baude and Stephen Sachs argue that, because our legal system is originalist as a matter of positive law, that is sufficient to justify originalism. Assuming judges must follow "the law," that means they must be originalist because originalism is part of our law already. That is, interpreting law through original public meaning is our society's "rule of recognition" – we collectively recognize the rule that laws are ordinarily interpreted with their original public meanings. This theory is rooted in the positivist account of law put forward most famously by H. L. A. Hart in his seminal work *The Concept of Law.* For an introduction to this theory, see William Baude, *Is Originalism Our Law?* 115 COLUM. L. REV. 2349 (2015) and Stephen E. Sachs, *Originalism as a Theory of Legal Change,* 38 HARV. J.L. & PUB. POL'Y 817 (2015). For a response to these theories, see Charles L. Barzun, The Positive U-Turn (Stanford Law Review forthcoming).

The implication of this theory, however, is that if, as a matter of social fact, our rule of recognition were something other than interpreting law through original public meaning, then judges should not be originalist. The question then becomes which rule *should* be our rule of recognition, i.e., how should we interpret legal rules in our society? If you agree that the "rule of law" values served by our existing rule of recognition are desirable, then, according to Baude and Sachs, that's all one needs to justify originalism. Thus, this theory is just another way of stating what we have stated here: (1) we interpret all law through original public meaning, (2) there are good reasons we do so in our legal system, and (3) whether what the original Constitution says is good or whether it has to be amended or perhaps abandoned is a separate inquiry.

Nonoriginalists respond that originalism is *not* our law – that those who decide legal questions in our society use nonoriginalist interpretations all the time. The reader can decide for him or herself whether our legal system is nonoriginalist, but keep in mind two things. First, "originalism" doesn't mean that *only* the original public meaning matters; we have already seen how other legal rules interact with original public meaning. But moreover, to the extent nonoriginalist interpretations of law exist in our legal system today, the reason is largely because of the movement by more progressive jurists in the twentieth century that I described in the previous chapter and to which originalism grew as a response. Historically our system has been originalist; that progressive jurists have tried to change that in recent years does not mean our legal system writ large has changed.

19 Jack Balkin shows how many conservative originalists believe that original expected applications are often the best evidence of original meaning. BALKIN, *supra* note 9, at 100–01, 104–08. To the extent his work earlier leaves the impression that modern-day conservative originalists believe (or at least that Justice Scalia believed) that only original expected applications are valid, *see id.* at 6–7, I think his later discussion better captures how most modern originalists think about expected applications.

20 Christopher R. Green, *Originalism and the Sense-Reference Distinction*, 50 ST. LOUIS U. L.J. 555 (2006).

21 H. Jefferson Powell, *The Original Understanding of Original Intent*, 98 HARV. L. REV. 885, 903 (1985).

22 *Id.* at 903–04.

23 Caleb Nelson, *Originalism and Interpretive Conventions*, 70 U. CHI. L. REV. 519, 536 & nn. 74–76 (2013) (quoting three letters from James Madison to various correspondents) (emphasis added).

24 DENNIS J. GOLDFORD, THE AMERICAN CONSTITUTION AND THE DEBATE OVER ORIGINALISM 63 (2005) (quoting Letter from James Madison to Henry Lee (June 25, 1824)).

25 Nelson, *supra* note 23, at 536.

26 *Id.* (quoting EMMERICH DE VATTEL, THE LAW OF NATIONS 202 (Charles G. Fenwick, trans., Carnegie Institution 1916) (1758)).

27 Nelson, *supra* note 23, at 536–37 (quoting 2 THOMAS RUTHERFORTH, INSTITUTES OF NATURAL LAW 336–37 (Bentham 2d ed. 1756)).

28 DAVID P. CURRIE, THE CONSTITUTION IN CONGRESS: DEMOCRATS AND WHIGS, 1829–1861, at xiii (2005).

29 THE FEDERALIST NO. 37, at 223–25 (James Madison) (Clinton Rossiter ed., 1961) (emphasis omitted).

3 CONSTITUTIONAL LEGITIMACY

1 THE DECLARATION OF INDEPENDENCE para. 2 (U.S. 1776).

2 The next two chapters are adapted and expanded from a prior law review article of mine. *See* Ilan Wurman, *The Original Understanding of Constitutional Legitimacy*, 2014 BYU L. REV. 819 (2015).

3 RANDY E. BARNETT, RESTORING THE LOST CONSTITUTION: THE PRESUMPTION OF LIBERTY 4 (2004); *see also id.* at 11–52.

4 *Id.* at 4.

5 Alex Kozinski, *Natural Law Jurisprudence: A Skeptical Perspective*, 36 HARV. J.L. PUB. POL´Y 977, 978 (2013).

6 ALLAN BLOOM, THE CLOSING OF THE AMERICAN MIND 39 (1987).

7 BARNETT, *supra* note 3, at 57.

8 *Id.* at 58.

9 JOHN LOCKE, TWO TREATISES OF GOVERNMENT 269–78 (Peter Laslett ed., 1988) (1690).

10 RICHARD A. EPSTEIN, TAKINGS: PRIVATE PROPERTY AND THE POWER OF EMINENT DOMAIN 14–15 (1985).

11 *Id.* at 15.

12 JACK BALKIN, LIVING ORIGINALISM 6–7 (2001); *see id.* at 24 ("[The] basic job [of constitutions] is not to prevent future decision-making but to enable it.").

13 *See* Antonin Scalia, *Common Law Courts in a Civil Law System: The Role of United States Federal Courts in Interpreting the Constitution and Laws*, in A MATTER OF INTERPRETATION: FEDERAL COURTS AND THE LAW 40–41 (Amy Gutmann ed., 1997).

14 BALKIN, *supra* note 12, at 4.

15 *Id.* at 11.

16 *Id.* at 55.

17 *Id.* at 64–73; *see also id.* at 71 ("The democratic legitimacy of the Constitution depends on the people's belief that their Constitution and their government belongs to them, so that if they speak and protest and make their views known over time, the constitutional construction of courts and the political branches will eventually respond to their political values and to the issues they care about most."). Balkin elaborates on this kind of legitimacy toward the end of his book. He insists that watershed cases such as *Brown v. Board* or the sexual equality cases of the 1970s followed on the heels of democratic and social movements, and thus his version of "democratic constitutionalism" is in fact democratically legitimate. *See id.* at 320–25.

18 JOHN HART ELY, DEMOCRACY AND DISTRUST 88 (1980).

19 *Id.* at 80, 82, 89, 92.

20 *Id.* at 87–88, 88–89 n.*.

21 SANFORD LEVINSON, OUR UNDEMOCRATIC CONSTITUTION 6–7 (2006).

22 Michael W. McConnell, *The Importance of Humility in Judicial Review: A Comment on Ronald Dworkin's 'Moral Reading' of the Constitution*, 65 FORDHAM L. REV. 1269, 1291 (1996–1997).

23 *See* Scalia, *supra* note 13, at 38.

24 *See* KEITH E. WHITTINGTON, CONSTITUTIONAL INTERPRETATION: TEXTUAL MEANING, ORIGINAL INTENT, AND JUDICIAL REVIEW 110–59 (1999).

25 *Id.* at 133.

26 *Id.* at 135.

27 THOMAS G. WEST, VINDICATING THE FOUNDERS, at xi (1997) (quoting CONOR CRUISE O'BRIEN, THE LONG AFFAIR: THOMAS JEFFERSON AND THE FRENCH REVOLUTION, 1785–1800, at 319 (1996)).

28 Paul A. Brest, *The Misconceived Quest for the Original Understanding*, 60 B.U. L. REV. 204, 230 (1980).

4 THE FOUNDERS ON FOUNDING

1 Letter from James Madison to Thomas Jefferson (Feb. 4, 1790), *in* THE MIND OF THE FOUNDER: SOURCES OF THE POLITICAL THOUGHT OF JAMES MADISON 176, 177 (Marvin Meyers ed., rev. ed. 1981) (emphasis in original).

2 For a summary of the progressive literature making this argument, see ALAN GIBSON, INTERPRETING THE FOUNDING: GUIDE TO THE ENDURING DEBATES OVER THE ORIGINS AND FOUNDATIONS OF THE AMERICAN REPUBLIC 9–11 (2006). Martin Diamond also discusses this argument in his essay on the Federalist. *See* Martin Diamond, *Democracy and the Federalist: A Reconsideration of the Framers' Intent*, 53 AM. POL. SCI. REV. Mar. 1959, at 52, 53.

3 THE FEDERALIST NO. 40, at 249 (James Madison) (Clinton Rossiter ed., 1961) (emphasis omitted).

4 BERNARD BAILYN, THE IDEOLOGICAL ORIGINS OF THE AMERICAN REVOLUTION 321–79 (Enlarged Ed. 1992).

5 THE DECLARATION OF INDEPENDENCE para. 5 (U.S. 1776).

6 *Id.* at para. 6.

7 *Id.* at para. 7.

8 *Id.* at para. 8.

9 *Id.* at para. 13, 19.

10 JOHN HART ELY, DEMOCRACY AND DISTRUST 49 (1980).

11 THE FEDERALIST NO. 39 (James Madison), *supra* note 3, at 236.

12 John Adams, *Thoughts on Government*, *in* THE POLITICAL WRITINGS OF JOHN ADAMS 83, 86 (George A. Peek, Jr., ed., 1954).

13 GORDON S. WOOD, THE CREATION OF THE AMERICAN REPUBLIC: 1776–1787, at 47 (1988) (1969).

14 1 THE RECORDS OF THE FEDERAL CONVENTION OF 1787, at 48 (Max Farrand ed., 1966) (1911).

15 *Id.* at 49.

16 *Id.* at 51.

17 THE FEDERALIST NO. 10 (James Madison), *supra* note 3, at 76.

18 *Id.* at 78–79.

19 In *Federalist* No. 62 Madison is explicit on this point. He argues for the necessity of a bicameral legislature because "all single and numerous assemblies" have a propensity "to yield to the impulse of sudden and violent passions. . . . Examples on this subject might be cited without number; and from proceedings within the United States." THE FEDERALIST NO. 62 (James Madison), *supra* note 3, at 377.

20 *See, e.g.,* THE FEDERALIST NO. 63 (James Madison), *supra* note 3, at 382–83 (arguing that the Senate will protect the people "against their own temporary errors and delusions," and that in moments of temporary passion, "how salutary will be the interference of some temperate and respectable body of citizens" to check such passions "until reason, justice, and truth can regain their authority over the public mind?"). The consensus among the Framers was that the Senate would be the most effective check on the popular passions of the people: Mr. Dickenson argued that a Senate chosen by the state legislatures would protect the states against encroachments from the general government, 1 FARRAND, *supra* note 14, at 152–53, but also create a body of virtuous men, *id.* at 150. Mason believed that the Senate would protect both the states, *id.* at 407, and the wealthy, *id.* at 428. Madison agreed that the tendency to refine and enlarge the public views would be amplified in the Senate, which had the "advantage of favoring a select appointment." THE FEDERALIST NO. 62 (James Madison), *supra* note 3, at 375.

21 *See, e.g.,* THE FEDERALIST NO. 51 (James Madison), *supra* note 3, at 320 (arguing that in a federal system such as the one contemplated by the Constitution, "a double security arises to the rights of the people. The different governments will control each other, at the same time that each will be controlled by itself.").

22 *See, e.g., id.* at 319 (arguing that a separation of powers will let "ambition counteract ambition").

23 James Otis, *The Rights of the British Colonies Asserted and Proved* (1764), *in* ISAAC KRAMNICK & THEODORE J. LOWI, AMERICAN POLITICAL THOUGHT: A NORTON ANTHOLOGY 100, 102 (2009) (emphasis in original).

24 Samuel Adams, *The Rights of the Colonists* (1772), *in* KRAMNICK & LOWI, *supra* note 23, at 108, 109 (emphasis in original).

25 Thomas Paine, *Common Sense* (1776), *in* KRAMNICK & LOWI, *supra* note 23, at 131, 132.

26 Alexander Hamilton, *The Farmer Refuted* (1775), *in* THE PAPERS OF ALEX-
   ANDER HAMILTON (Harold C. Syrett et al., eds., 1961–79), http://press-
   pubs.uchicago.edu/founders/documents/v1ch3s5.html.

27 Thomas Tudor Tucker, *Conciliatory Hints, Attempting by a Fair State of
   Matters, to Remove Party Prejudice* (1784), *quoted in* WOOD, *supra* note 13,
   at 280–81.

28 WOOD, *supra* note 13, at 281.

29 THE FEDERALIST NO. 38 (James Madison), *supra* note 3, at 231.

30 THE FEDERALIST NO. 1 (Alexander Hamilton), *supra* note 3, at 27.

31 THE FEDERALIST NO. 49 (James Madison), *supra* note 3, at 310.

32 THE FEDERALIST NO. 39 (James Madison), *supra* note 3, at 239–40.

33 THE FEDERALIST NO. 43 (James Madison), *supra* note 3, at 275.

34 *See* THE FEDERALIST NO. 22 (Alexander Hamilton), *supra* note 3, at 148.

35 THE FEDERALIST NO. 40 (James Madison), *supra* note 3, at 248.

36 *Id.* at 249 (emphasis in original).

37 James Wilson, Pennsylvania Ratifying Convention (Dec. 4, 1787), *quoted in*
   DANIEL A. FARBER & SUZANNA SHERRY, A HISTORY OF THE AMERICAN
   CONSTITUTION 276 (2d. ed. 2005) (emphasis in original).

38 FARBER & SHERRY , *supra* note 37, at 48.

39 *See id.* at 50 (Madison arguing that "the new Constitution should be ratified
   in the most unexceptionable form, and by the supreme authority of the
   people themselves").

40 *Id.*

41 *See* WOOD, *supra* note 13, at 268–91.

42 *Id.* at 274.

43 *Id.* at 276.

44 *See, e.g.*, JACK BALKIN, LIVING ORIGINALISM 41–44 (2011) (explaining the
   dead hand argument and how his theory solves it); DAVID A. STRAUSS, THE
   LIVING CONSTITUTION 99–104 (2010); John O. McGinnis & Michael B.
   Rappaport, *Our Supermajoritarian Constitution*, 80 TEX. L. REV. 703,
   796–97 (2002).

45 Letter from Thomas Jefferson to James Madison (Sept. 6, 1789), *in* THE
   ESSENTIAL JEFFERSON 176, 176 (Jean M. Yarbrough ed., 2006) (emphasis
   in original).

46 Letter from James Madison to Thomas Jefferson (Feb. 4, 1790), *in* THE
   MIND OF THE FOUNDER: SOURCES OF THE POLITICAL THOUGHT OF JAMES
   MADISON 176, 177 (Marvin Meyers ed., rev. ed. 1981) (emphasis in
   original).

47 THE FEDERALIST NO. 37 (James Madison), *supra* note 3, at 226.

48 *Id.* at 227.

49 THE FEDERALIST NO. 38 (James Madison), *supra* note 3, at 229.

50 THE FEDERALIST NO. 37 (James Madison), *supra* note 3, at 223.

51 THE FEDERALIST NO. 49 (James Madison), *supra* note 3, at 312.

52 *Id.* at 311 (emphasis added).

53 Thomas Tudor Tucker made this same observation. Only a constitution rooted in the collective will of the people "would have the most promising chance of stability." WOOD, *supra* note 13, at 281.

54 THE DECLARATION OF INDEPENDENCE para. 1 (U.S. 1776) ("When in the Course of human events, it becomes necessary for one people to dissolve the political bands which have connected them with another, and to assume among the powers of the earth, the separate and equal station to which the Laws of Nature and of Nature's God entitle them, a decent respect to the opinions of mankind requires that they should declare the causes which impel them to the separation.").

55 *Id.* at para. 2.

56 On this revolutionary ideology, the best work may still be BAILYN, *supra* note 4. On the tensions between this ideology and the framing and ratifying of the Constitution, see in particular pages 321–79.

57 THE FEDERALIST NO. 14 (James Madison), *supra* note 3, at 99.

58 This approach is similar to the theory of originalism advanced by John McGinnis and Michael Rappaport. They argue that because the original Constitution was adopted by supermajorities and garnered widespread acceptance, it is likely a better Constitution than could otherwise have been obtained through processes that did not require supermajority approval. Thus, to obtain these better consequences, we must be originalist because it is the *original* Constitution that these supermajorities enacted. This theory, and the approach I just described in the text, stand or fall with the normative claim that the Constitution as originally understood happens to be a good constitution. For further reading, see John McGinnis & Michael Rappaport, *Originalism and the Good Constitution*, 98 GEO. L.J. 1693 (2010), or their book of the same title, JOHN O. MCGINNIS & MICHAEL B. RAPPAPORT, ORIGINALISM AND THE GOOD CONSTITUTION (2013).

5 INTERPRETING THE CONSTITUTION

1 Gompers v. United States, 233 U.S. 604, 610 (1914).

2 Gary Lawson made such an argument in terms of burdens of proof. Gary Lawson, *Legal Indeterminacy: Its Causes and Cure*, 19 HARV. J.L. & PUB. POL'Y 411, 423–28 (1995).

3 The most authoritative statement is Lawrence B. Solum, *The Interpretation-Construction Distinction*, 27 CONST. COMMENT. 95 (2010).

4 Ashwander v. TVA, 297 U.S. 288, 354 (1934).

5 James B. Thayer, *The Origin and Scope of the American Doctrine of Constitutional Law*, 7 HARV. L. REV. 129, 144 (1893).

6 Robert H. Bork, *Neutral Principles and Some First Amendment Problems*, 47 IND. L.J. 1, 11 (1971).

7 In particular, Michael McConnell has implied that the will of the people ought to be entitled to presumptive validity. Michael McConnell, *The Importance of Humility in Judicial Review: A Comment on Ronald Dworkin's Moral Reading of the Constitution*, 65 FORDHAM L. REV. 1269, 1291 (1997). Kurt Lash's theory of the Ninth Amendment – which, he argues, reflects the Founders' commitments to federalism and popular sovereignty – would lead to a presumption of constitutionality of state legislative acts restricting rights. *See, e.g.*, Kurt T. Lash, *On Federalism, Freedom, and the Founders' View of Retained Rights*, 60 STAN. L. REV. 969, 972 (2008) (arguing that the Ninth Amendment was meant to give states discretion with respect to "retained rights"); Kurt T. Lash, *Of Inkblots and Originalism: Historical Ambiguity and the Case of the Ninth Amendment*, 31 HARV. J.L. & PUB. POL'Y 467, 472 (2008) ("The proper stance of an originalist judge in the face of historical ambiguity, then, is one of humility. If the original meaning of the text remains obscured, then courts lack authority to use the text to interfere with the political process. Put another way, in a case of historical ambiguity, the very legitimacy of judicial review is obscured – as if by an inkblot."). Michael Stokes Paulsen writes that the meaning of the language is indeterminate or under-determinate when applied to a specific case, then typically the "political decisions made by an imperfect representative democracy" can prevail. Michael Stokes Paulsen, *How to Interpret the Constitution (and How Not To)*, 115 YALE L.J. 2037, 2057 (2006).

8 Lino A. Graglia, *Originalism and the Constitution: Does Originalism Always Provide the Answer?*, 34 HARV. J.L. PUB. POL'Y 73, 85 (2011).

9 *See* TIMOTHY SANDEFUR, THE CONSCIENCE OF THE CONSTITUTION: THE DECLARATION OF INDEPENDENCE AND THE RIGHT TO LIBERTY (2013).

10 Collin Levy, *Litigating for Liberty*, WALL ST. J. (Jan. 7, 2012), https://www.wsj.com/articles/SB10001424052970203513604577144902274972614.

11 *See* RICHARD EPSTEIN, THE CLASSICAL LIBERAL CONSTITUTION (2014); *see also* Richard Epstein, *Preface* to ROBERT A. LEVY & WILLIAM MELLOR, THE DIRTY DOZEN, at xviii (2008).

12 RANDY E. BARNETT, RESTORING THE LOST CONSTITUTION: THE PRESUMPTION OF LIBERTY 152 (2004); *see also id.* at 153–90 (Necessary and Proper Clause); *id.* at 191–203 (Privileges or Immunities Clause); *id.* at 235–42 (Ninth Amendment); *id.* at 278–318 (Commerce Clause).

13 *Id.* at 260.

14 EPSTEIN, CLASSICAL LIBERAL CONSTITUTION, *supra* note 11, at 53–54.

15 John O. McGinnis & Michael Rappaport, *Original Methods Originalism*, 103 NW. U. L. REV. 751, 773 (2009).

16 *Id.* at 774.

17 Caleb Nelson, *Originalism and Interpretive Conventions*, 70 U. CHI. L. REV 519, 576–78 (2003).

18 1 JOSEPH STORY, COMMENTARIES ON THE CONSTITUTION OF THE UNITED STATES 383 (Forgotten Books 2015) (1833).

19 Nelson, *supra* note 17, 575–76 (2003) (quoting 1 BLACKSTONE'S COMMENTARIES: WITH NOTES OF REFERENCE, TO THE CONSTITUTION AND LAWS, OF THE FEDERAL GOVERNMENT OF THE UNITED STATES; AND OF THE COMMONWEALTH OF VIRGINIA app D, at 151 [Lawbook Exchange 1996] [St. George Tucker, ed., 1803]).

20 Letter from Thomas Jefferson to Wilson Cary Nicholas (Sept. 7, 1803), *in* THE ESSENTIAL JEFFERSON 203, 204 (Jean M. Yarbrough ed., 2006).

21 Gibbons v. Ogden, 22 U.S. (9 Wheat.) 1, 187–89.

22 STORY, *supra* note 18, at 418–19.

23 McGinnis and Rappaport, *supra* note 15, at 775 ("There is evidence that, in the early republic, when two interpretations were equally plausible, judges were required to assume the constitutionality of the legislation.").

24 John O. McGinnis, *The Duty of Clarity*, 84 GEO. WASH. L. REV. 843, 880–908, 908–09 (2016).

25 1 WILLIAM BLACKSTONE, COMMENTARIES ON THE LAWS OF ENGLAND *60 (emphasis in original).

26 STORY, *supra* note 18, at 387.

27 THE FEDERALIST NO. 37, at 223–25 (James Madison) (Clinton Rossiter ed., 1961); *see also* Nelson, *supra* note 17, at 525–36. As this book goes to press, William Baude is working on what promises to be one of the definitive articles on the concept of liquidation. William Baude, Constitutional Liquidation (Jan. 29, 2017) (unpublished manuscript) (on file with author).

28 DAVID P. CURRIE, THE CONSTITUTION IN CONGRESS: THE FEDERALIST PERIOD, 1789–1801, at 116 (1997) (quoting 1 ANNALS OF CONGRESS 514 [Gales & Seaton, eds., 1834] [hereinafter "ANNALS"]).

29 DAVID P. CURRIE, THE CONSTITUTION IN CONGRESS: THE JEFFERSONIANS, 1801–1829, at 255 (2001) (quoting 28 ANNALS at 189–91).

30 CURRIE, THE FEDERALIST PERIOD, *supra* note 28, at 27 (quoting 1 ANNALS at 83).

31 Stuart v. Laird, 5 U.S. (1 Cranch) 299, 309, quoted in *id.* at 54.

32 Nelson, *supra* note 17, at 578–83.

33 Baude explains how this concept is distinct from the modern understanding of judicial precedents in that it required a "course" of several deliberate decisions and practices across numerous constitutional actors, and that it be understood to include the sanction of the people themselves, in favor of a particular outcome. Baude, *supra* note 27, at 10–14.

6 LAWYERS AS HISTORIANS

1 DAVID HACKETT FISCHER, HISTORIANS´ FALLACIES: TOWARD A LOGIC OF HISTORICAL THOUGHT 5 (1970).

2 This chapter is adapted from a longer law review article, Ilan Wurman, *Law Historians' Fallacies*, 91 N.D. L. REV. 161 (2015), and I thank the law review for permission to reuse this material.

3 DAVID STRAUSS, THE LIVING CONSTITUTION 18 (2010).

4 David Strauss, *Originalism, Conservatism, and Judicial Restraint*, 34 HARV. J.L. PUB. POL´Y 137, 140 (2011).

5 FISCHER, *supra* note 1.

6 Wurman, *supra* note 2, at 178–79, 186–88.

7 Stephen E. Sachs, *Originalism as a Theory of Legal Change*, 38 HARV. J.L. PUB. POL´Y 817, 887 (2015).

8 G. Edward White, *The Arrival of History in Constitutional Scholarship*, 88 VA. L. REV. 485, 506, 494 (2002).

9 LEO STRAUSS, NATURAL RIGHT AND HISTORY 16 (1965).

10 Quentin Skinner, *Meaning and Understanding in the History of Ideas*, 8 HIST. & THEORY 3, 6 (1969).

11 *Id.*

12 William E. Nelson, *History and Neutrality in Constitutional Adjudication*, 72 VA. L. REV. 1237, 1243 (1986).

13 *Id.* at 1244.

14 STRAUSS, *supra* note 9, at 24–25.

7 *BROWN V. BOARD* AND ORIGINALISM

1 David A. Strauss, *Can Originalism Be Saved?*, 92 B.U. L. REV. 1160, 1161 (2012).

2 Michael W. McConnell, *The Originalist Case for* Brown v. Board of Education, 19 HARV. J. L. PUB. POL´Y 457, 459 (1995) [hereinafter McConnell, *The Originalist Case*]. McConnell's much longer article making the case is 195 pages and culls significant historical evidence. *See* Michael W. McConnell, *Originalism and the Desegregation Decisions*, 81 VA. L. REV. 947 (1995) [hereinafter McConnell, *Desegregation Decisions*].

3 McConnell, *Desegregation Decisions*, *supra* note 2, at 980.

4 McConnell, *The Originalist Case*, *supra* note 2, at 463.

5 *Id.* at 464 (quoting 3 CONG. REC. 981 (1875) (remarks of Rep. Cain)).

6 McConnell, *The Originalist Case*, *supra* note 2, at 458.

7 McConnell, *Desegregation Decisions*, *supra* note 2, at 1093–1105.

8 Michael J. Klarman, Brown, *Originalism, and Constitutional Theory: A Response to Professor McConnell*, 81 VA. L. REV. 1881 (1995).

9 Michael W. McConnell, *The Originalist Justification for* Brown: *A Reply to Professor Klarman*, 81 VA. L. REV. 1937 (1995).

10 A new originalist defense of *Brown* was recently put forward by Steven Calabresi and Michael Perl. They argue that public education was

considered a civil right as of 1868, and therefore, because the Fourteenth Amendment was understood to guarantee blacks the same civil rights as whites, the right to a "common" public education along with whites was required by an original understanding of the Fourteenth Amendment. *See* Steven G. Calabresi & Michael W. Perl, *Originalism and* Brown v. Board of Education, 2014 MICH. ST. L. REV. 429 (2014). Although this is an interesting approach, it suffers from several potentially fatal arguments. No one disputes that the Fourteenth Amendment was intended to guarantee the civil rights of blacks, but not necessarily their political or social rights; and it may even be that public education was considered a civil right (though this, too, is controversial). Further, no one disputes that the amendment enshrined a racial nondiscrimination principle. The biggest problem with Calabresi and Perl is that they simply presume the conclusion that, because public education was a civil right, this meant *desegregated* public education was a civil right. The whole question, however, is whether the separate-but-equal doctrine is an acceptable nondiscrimination principle or not. It strikes me that Calabresi and Perl's approach is rather question-begging. Even they recognize that the state constitutions on which they rely are almost entirely silent on the question of segregation, which to me suggests that, by their own approach, the Fourteenth Amendment did not constitutionalize one way or another a right for segregated or desegregated schools. I think McConnell's approach is more persuasive.

11 ROBERT H. BORK, THE TEMPTING OF AMERICA: THE POLITICAL SEDUCTION OF THE LAW 82 (1990).

12 Christopher R. Green, *Originalism and the Sense-Reference Distinction*, 50 ST. LOUIS U. L.J. 555, 605 (2006).

13 *Id.* at 619.

8 A CODA ON NONORIGINALISMS

1 Gompers v. United States, 233 U.S. 604, 610 (1914).

2 DAVID A. STRAUSS, THE LIVING CONSTITUTION 100–01 (2010).

3 MARK A. GRABER, A NEW INTRODUCTION TO AMERICAN CONSTITUTIONALISM 40–64 (2013).

4 There are many secondary sources one may consult on English legal history, but for the nature of the common law and its relationship to statute law one can simply consult Blackstone's chapter "Of the laws of England." 1 WILLIAM BLACKSTONE, COMMENTARIES ON THE LAWS OF ENGLAND *62–91. See especially where he explains that statutes may be "declaratory" of the common law or "remedial" of its defects. *Id.* at *86. For parliamentary supremacy, *see id.* at *160–61.

5 STRAUSS, *supra* note 2, at 43–46.

6 RONALD DWORKIN, FREEDOM'S LAW: THE MORAL READING OF THE
AMERICAN CONSTITUTION 17 (1996).

7 *Id.* at 24–26.

8 *Id.* at 32.

9 *See, e.g.*, James Fleming, *The Natural Rights-Based Justification for Judicial
Review*, 69 FORDHAM L. REV. 2119, 2129 & n.61 (noting this criticism of
Dworkin's "happy endings" and crediting Sandy Levinson with the criticism); *Fidelity As Integrity: Colloquy*, 65 FORDHAM L. REV. 1357, 1358
(1997) (where Sandy Levinson notes that he had "criticized [Dworkin] in
the past for having a predilection for happy endings").

10 Dworkin noted that it had been "said that the results I claim for the moral
reading, in particular constitutional cases, magically coincide with those
I favor politically myself." DWORKIN, *supra* note 6, at 36. For the most part,
Dworkin concedes and even embraces this criticism, stating, "I not only
concede but emphasize that constitutional opinion is sensitive to political
conviction." *Id.* at 37. He does attempt to rebut some of the criticism,
however, by claiming that his preferred constitution would require redistri-
bution of wealth but his moral reading of the Constitution does not require it.
Id. at 36. But of course there is nothing that would stop the political branches,
according to Dworkin's interpretation of the Constitution, from redistrib-
uting wealth should they want to do so. That hardly seems a sacrifice. He
also argues that he does not "admire or approve" flag burners or pornog-
raphers, although he thinks the Constitution defends theirs rights. *Id.* But that
subtly changes the question. His political commitments require that free
speech of that kind be protected. And his constitutional interpretation always
supports that result. That he does not "approve or admire" of flag burners
does not seem to rebut the criticism. That would be a different kind of
commitment.

11 *Id.* at 2.

12 *See* JOHN HART ELY, DEMOCRACY AND DISTRUST 43–72 (1980).

13 *Id.* at 74.

14 *Id.* at 88.

15 *Id.* at 100.

16 *See* STRAUSS, *supra* note 2, at 8.

17 Caleb Nelson, *Sovereign Immunity as a Doctrine of Personal Jurisdiction*, 115
HARV. L. REV. 1559, 1565, 1567–1608 (2002).

18 *See, e.g.*, William Baude, *Sovereign Immunity and the Constitutional Text*,
103 VA. L. REV. 1, 8–9 (2017).

19 STRAUSS, *supra* note 2, at 107.

EPILOGUE

1 This story is taken from PAULINE MAIER, RATIFICATION: THE PEOPLE DEBATE THE CONSTITUTION, 1787–1788, at 144–45 (2010).
2 THE FEDERALIST NO. 1, at 27 (Alexander Hamilton) (Clinton Rossiter ed., 1961).
3 *See* Treaty Establishing a Constitution for Europe, 2004 O.J. (C 310).

INDEX